Second Printing, 2024

THURSTON M. SMITH &
JAIMEL D. HILL

TO BE ONE HE HAS TO SEE ONE

THE ONLY WAY A BOY BECOMES A RIGHTEOUS MAN

Alpha Gentleman Lifestyle Development

We dedicate this work to all fathers past, present, and future, as well as to our families who believe in our mission and vision. And the ancestors who made it possible for us to be here inspired us to wear the mantle and carry the torch of fatherhood, to be beacons of light and lead in the way God has ordained us. We pray this book serves you well. To our mentors, friends, and fellow travelers, know that your influence permeates every word. We are humbled to stand on the shoulders of giants, offering this work to you with profound gratitude and respect.

Thurston M. Smith
(Alpha Gentleman Lifestyle Development)

Jaimel D. Hill
(#DBWT - Don't Be Wasted Talent)

CONTENTS

CONTENTS

PROLOGUE

ALWAYS BE TRUE

There's one thing a man should always do.
Mainly to himself be true.
Never let anyone change your point of view.
Unless what he brings makes sense to you.
You should never judge him by the sight alone.
Or by the height that he has grown.
And when you're speaking.
Always keep a moderate tone.
Because of raised voices, they turn their hearts to stone.
See, from the beginning, it was brother killing brother,
and the morals in life are to
live, love, and respect one another.
Then there are those that'll be evilly smart.
They'll take a decent man and alter his heart.
Until he seeks to tear them apart.
These men, no man should call friends.
They bend lies around truths until they meet their end.

TO BE ONE HE HAS TO
SEE ONE

UNDERSTANDING THE FATHERHOOD LANDSCAPE

In exploring the vital role of fathers in guiding their sons from boyhood to manhood, we get to the core of fatherhood and its profound societal impact. Starting with the significant figures that sketch the landscape of American fatherhood, we uncover stories behind the statistics that resonate with the challenges and triumphs of fathering.

America, home to approximately 72.2 million fathers, presents a mosaic of fatherhood narratives. Divorced fathers comprise 44%, unmarried 33%, separated 19%, and widowed 4.2%. Our hearts extend to those grappling with loss; their grief is a heart-rending reminder of the fragility of human connections. These figures illuminate the diverse pathways of fatherhood, each carrying its challenges and impacts on children and society. The narrative extends beyond numbers. You and I are a part of these particular stats in these national narratives, as these numbers affect and influence our communities. This information has affected us and how we grew up, and is now impacting the families, which are your children and spouse, and the broader social spectrum being your neighborhood and beyond, as these stats come from an individual decision as well as a group decision of two or more.

A Fathers Behvaior

The ripple effect of individual actions, akin to dominos in an intricate setup, can either uphold or undermine the societal structure. Fathers' behaviors have far-reaching consequences, and this interconnectedness means that personal choices reverberate, impacting others in seen and unseen ways. This aligns with the adage, "Society is only as strong as the family," emphasizing the family's pivotal role in societal health. And that is based on a Father's behavior. So, what does that look like, and how would it be explained?

One way to explain it is with the concept of "six degrees of separation," first introduced by Frigyes Karinthy in 1929 and later popularized by psychologist Stanley Milgram, which suggests that we are all just six or fewer interpersonal connections away from each other. This web of social ties creates a complex network where the actions of individuals, particularly those in influential roles such as fathers, have ripple effects that can be felt far beyond their immediate circles. The behaviors of fathers, serving as the cornerstone of familial structures, often extend beyond the confines of the home, influencing the community and, by extension, society at large.

Renowned psychologist Erik Erikson postulated that a father's identity and role within the family contribute significantly to children's psychological development. Erikson's stages of psychosocial development suggest that a father's presence and behavior can profoundly affect a child's sense of trust, autonomy, and initiativeness, shaping their future interactions and societal contributions. As the child's concept of interpersonal relationships forms, it carries the imprints of these paternal behaviors into a broader societal context.

The father's role in anthropology is often seen as vital in transmitting cultural norms and values. Claude Lévi-Strauss, a leading anthropologist, argued that family and kinship structures play a crucial role in organizing societies. Under their roles, fathers participate in perpetuating or transforming these structures. Thus, their behaviors can either uphold or challenge the existing social fabric, affecting the community in ways that may not be immediately apparent but are nonetheless significant.

And that brings us back to the adage, "Society is only as strong as the family," which echoes through the teachings of various religious traditions, where the father's role is central. For instance, in Christianity, the Apostle Paul in Ephesians 6:4 advises fathers to bring up their children "in the training and instruction of the Lord," highlighting fatherhood's spiritual and moral dimensions. In Islam, the Prophet Muhammad (PBUH) says, "The best of you is the best to his family," emphasizing the importance of paternal conduct in society's overall health. These religious perspectives underscore the ethical and moral ripples that a father's behavior can create within the larger community.

Social science also reveals the far-reaching effects of fathers' actions. Urie Bronfenbrenner's ecological systems theory illustrates how individual development is affected by the different systems of relationships in which they participate. The family, and within it the father's role, is a primary microsystem that interacts with larger societal systems, influencing and being influenced by the broader expanse of the child's experiences.

Let's simplify this. Imagine a set of those Russian nesting dolls, where each doll opens up to reveal another smaller one inside. Like those dolls, we all live in an extensive system of smaller systems. Urie Bronfenbrenner, an intelligent man who studied families and how people grow, thought about society like those nesting dolls. He said each person is like the most miniature doll, and they are part of a family, which is a little bit bigger doll. This family is the first system we know, and it's super important because it's where we start learning about the world. The father is a significant part of this family system. How a dad acts and behaves and what he teaches his children can shape their thoughts, feelings, and behavior.

Like a hand in a glove, the family fits inside even bigger systems like schools, communities, and the world. So, when Dad does something, he's moving one piece of the big puzzle and making such an impact that his actions can affect not just his children but all the other pieces around him, even those that seem far away. It's like dropping a pebble in the water, and the ripples spread far and wide. That's how a dad's behavior can reach out and touch many people, even those he doesn't know. This helps us to understand that the behaviors of fathers or male figures in society have extensive consequences that align with the principle of "six degrees of separation." Their influence permeates through intimate relationships with the global community, reinforcing the notion that the vibrancy and resilience of society are deeply intertwined with the health and functionality of the family unit. Fathers' actions are not insular; they are woven into the fabric of social reality, affecting generations and social structures in profound ways that reflect the interconnectedness of human experience.

Divorce and Separation.

These are not just disruptions of a marital union; they are catalysts for a cascade of negative repercussions—economic strife, psychological wounds, and community disintegration. Research outlines that boys without a father or the environment of a stable marriage are more prone to aggressive behaviors—both **reactive-expressive**, like verbal and physical outbursts, and **reactive-inexpressive**, characterized by hostility.

And then there is what we call "**positive aggression**." Positive aggression is not a formal psychological term; instead, it's a colloquial way of describing a type of assertive behavior that is proactive and directed toward achieving positive outcomes without causing harm or infringing on the rights of others. The concept is derived from the broader psychological understanding of aggression, which traditionally has a negative connotation associated with hostility, anger, and the potential for violence or destruction.

However, constructively channeling aggressive energy has gained traction in various contexts, such as sports, business, or personal development. This reinterpreted "positive aggression" refers to the drive, determination, and forcefulness used to overcome obstacles, pursue goals, and improve oneself or one's situation without the negative impact typically associated with aggressive behavior.

When simplified to male behavior, positive aggression is a socially acceptable way for men to express their innate drive and assertiveness. It can be linked to traditional gender roles encouraging men to be competitive, decisive, and strong. In many societies, these traits are celebrated as part of masculinity. When expressed constructively rather than destructively, positive aggression can lead to success in various domains, such as sports, leadership, and personal challenges.

You also see positive aggression in the dynamic of a healthy marriage – assertiveness, boundary-setting, emotional control, and confident pursuit of goals. Such traits are cultivated through constructive channels and are best mirrored in a nurturing father-son relationship. However, divorce, separation, or parental absence can curtail these vital lessons. Positive aggression is essential, and its role extends across life's arenas, enabling effective navigation of social, professional, and personal spheres with intention and dignity. When balanced with mutual respect and empathy, it fosters successful outcomes and sustains solid and healthy relationships.

However, when the checks and balances of emotional control and empathy are eroded, positive aggression can swiftly morph into hostile aggression. This transition often occurs when assertiveness crosses the line into hostility, when establishing boundaries becomes rigid and exclusionary, and when the pursuit of goals disregards the well-being and rights of others. Hostile aggression manifests as behaviors that are no longer about self-respect and goal attainment but rather about domination, control, and, often, the infliction of emotional or physical harm. In the absence of a role model, such as through parental separation or divorce, the individual may lack the necessary guidance to modulate their assertiveness and ambition, leading to an imbalance where aggression overshadows restraint and respect for others. Furthermore, the trauma from such family disruptions can engender feelings of insecurity and anger, fueling a propensity towards aggressive behaviors as a misguided form of self-defense or compensatory control.

Positive aggression in the context of fatherhood can be seen as the assertive energy and proactive involvement a father exerts to engage with and guide his children. It is characterized by a keen attentiveness to the child's needs, clear communication, and a supportive presence. The transition from positive to negative aggression can occur when assertiveness turns into dominance, guidance into control, and attentiveness into intrusiveness, often fueled by frustration, misunderstanding, or stress. To maintain the balance and prevent the slide from positive to negative aggression, a father might employ the following strategies:

Active Listening: Instead of imposing his expectations, a father can practice active listening, which validates the child's feelings and perspectives and fosters mutual respect.

Empathy: By empathizing with his child, a father can respond to misbehavior with understanding rather than punitive measures.

Consistent Discipline: Positive aggression involves setting boundaries and consequences consistently and fairly without resorting to harshness or anger.

Role Modeling (*being the real model*): Demonstrating how to handle conflict and stress constructively teaches children to do the same.

Positive Reinforcement: Encouraging and rewarding good behavior is a hallmark of positive aggression, as opposed to using fear or intimidation to enforce rules.

Real-Life Example:

Consider a father who coaches his son's soccer team. He demonstrates positive aggression by being assertive in coaching, providing clear instructions, and encouraging hard work. He sets high expectations for his son and the team but balances this with encouragement and recognition of their efforts and improvements, regardless of the outcome of their games.

One day, his son misses a critical goal, and the team loses the match. The father could develop hostile aggression by criticizing his son harshly, leading to resentment and decreased self-esteem. Instead, he focuses on what his son did well during the game. He discusses what can be learned from the missed opportunity, maintaining a positive influence and helping his son build resilience.

In the broader landscape of fatherhood, this balanced approach to positive aggression can significantly influence a child's development, particularly after family separation. Fathers who manage this balance can help their children navigate the complexities of their emotions and social challenges, ultimately contributing to better behavior and emotional health outcomes.

Understanding The Fatherhood Landscape

Understanding the fatherhood landscape requires acknowledging the intricate balance between being a firm guide and a nurturing presence. Fathers are called to step into this role with a mindful approach, harnessing their strength and passion to foster their children's growth and well-being. The true mark of positive aggression in fatherhood is the legacy of resilience, empathy, and emotional intelligence it instills in the next generation.

Let this be the call to action: Fathers, embrace the positive aggression that builds rather than breaks, that guides rather than goads. In doing so, you will become the architects of a healthier, more emotionally mighty future for your children.

The landscape of American fatherhood is as varied as it is vast, containing an anthology of experiences that shape the nation's social fabric. For boys, the absence or presence of their fathers can mark the compass of their journey toward manhood.

Broken family setups, which include all the different kinds of families we see today, have been linked to more trouble-making and mental health issues in young boys. Schools and friend groups, where kids show what they're about, feel the impact of these family problems. However, even in these tough situations, using one's energy positively and assertively can be a helpful guide.

Scholars like Amato & Gilbreth, Anguiano, and Menning's research illuminates the profound impact of a father's role in mitigating the adverse effects of family fragmentation. Their findings echo through the halls of academia and resonate within therapeutic conversations addressing the welfare of children. These researchers have drawn the map that leads us from the shadow of separation toward the potential of engaged fatherhood.

In conclusion, we see the potential for greatness, guidance, and the molding of a generation of boys who will learn to navigate their aggressions positively. To be a man of resilience and character, a boy has to see one, and therein lies the unspoken power of fatherhood.

The critical role of fathers in the upbringing of children, particularly in the context of masculinity and fatherhood, is a subject that often doesn't receive the attention it deserves. The prevailing notion is that children should maintain a dynamic relationship with their fathers. Yet, this concept is only sometimes fully understood or valued by society. Significant, well-documented consequences are associated with the breakdown of family structures, mainly affecting boys. These include a propensity towards delinquent behavior and a decrease in mental health. Educational achievements may suffer, and the ability to form and maintain social relationships can be compromised.

However, the evidence suggests that when fathers remain actively involved in their children's lives after separation, many harmful impacts can be diminished. Active and positive father engagement has been linked to better behavioral and emotional outcomes in children. This positive effect of a father's involvement has been supported by research from scholars such as Amato & Gilbreth (1999), Anguiano (2004), and Menning (2002, 2006), indicating that the presence of a caring father figure plays a vital role in mitigating the challenges faced by children from separated families.

In light of the evidence, it becomes clear that the presence and involvement of fathers play a pivotal role in the well-being and development of children, particularly in the aftermath of family separation. The research underscores the significant positive impact that active fathering has on minimizing the adverse effects traditionally associated with broken homes. This reaffirms the importance of reevaluating and supporting the role of fathers in today's ever-changing family structures.

As we conclude this portion of the exploration of the fatherhood landscape, it's evident that fathers are not just peripheral figures in their children's lives. Instead, they are central to providing the stability, love, and guidance children need to thrive, regardless of the family's configuration. The challenge now lies in breaking down societal barriers and outdated stereotypes that limit men's participation in their children's lives. This requires a collective effort from the legal system, societal norms, and individual families to recognize and facilitate the valuable contributions fathers can make.

Looking ahead, the future of fatherhood offers a hopeful vista. It's one where fathers are empowered and encouraged to engage deeply with their children, transcending traditional roles and embracing a more holistic approach to parenting. This shift benefits children and enriches the fathers' lives, fostering deeper connections and more fulfilling experiences in their parenting journey.

As society continues to evolve, so must our understanding and support of the role of fatherhood. By championing the importance of active and positive father engagement, we can work towards a future where every child can grow up with the support of a loving and involved father. This vision not only brightens the prospects of individual families but strengthens the fabric of society as a whole, building a foundation of empathy, resilience, and mutual respect for generations to come.

WHAT IS A FATHER

Let's explore this role from a broader, more subtle perspective to clarify and deepen our understanding of fatherhood within our community.

The Oxford Languages Dictionary defines a father as a man in relation to his child or children, emphasizing biological paternity, care, and protection. While this definition provides a starting point, it merely scratches the surface of fatherhood's profound and complex nature. We must go beyond the surface-level descriptions to grasp the full depth of being a father.

The term' father' is profoundly explained in an enlightening sermon by Dr. Myles Munroe, which I felt compelled to reference in our discourse. Dr. Munroe predicates that the concept of 'father' is so significant that it is one of the titles the Creator ascribes to Himself, underscoring the divine origin and essence of fatherhood. This title is not used casually; it embodies many responsibilities and attributes.

The Hebrew word 'Abba,' which translates to 'father,' conveys a broad meaning: source, nourisher, sustainer, provider, protector, progenitor (forebear), foundation, founder, and author. These terms represent a function or role rather than a mere label. They paint a picture of a father as someone central to the life and well-being of their child, offering support in various forms—emotional, physical, and spiritual.

In discussing the creation narrative, Dr. Munroe reflects on the biblical account that God first created a male human from the soil. It was from this male being that a female was formed—not from the soil but from within the male. In this perspective, the male is seen as the source—the 'father'—of the female. While this viewpoint is steeped in religious doctrine and may not resonate with all belief systems, it offers an intriguing angle on the origins of the terms' father' and 'mother' within this particular theological framework. It's important to acknowledge that such interpretations are not universally held and that understanding fatherhood can vary widely across different cultures, religions, and individual beliefs. The essential takeaway is that fatherhood encompasses a spectrum of responsibilities and is not confined to biological progeny alone.

In exploring what it means to be a father, we must consider the role's broader implications. A father figure may provide guidance, wisdom, and a sense of security. He can also be a mentor, a teacher, and a steadfast pillar in the lives of his children or those he takes under his wing. This title is earned through actions and sustained by a commitment to nurture and guide.

As we educate our community on this subject, let's invite open dialogue and diverse perspectives, fostering a more profound understanding that transcends the basic definitions and embraces the sincere impact a father can have on individuals and society.

Society's expectations of gender roles are changing, often placing undue stress on women by expecting them to fulfill roles traditionally associated with men, such as being the primary provider or protector. This can lead to significant physical and emotional strain, potentially resulting in health issues that are not typically associated with women because these roles don't align with traditional expectations. Not only that, but they don't align with their physical-biological development in scientific understanding of women's health and well-being.

Research has indicated that the stress of balancing work and family responsibilities, particularly when combined with societal pressures to fulfill non-traditional roles, can have adverse effects on women's health. For instance, a study published in the *Journal of Occupational Health Psychology* found that women who experience high demands at work and home are at a greater risk of physical and mental health problems (Allen et al., 2000).

Additionally, the conflict between traditional gender roles and emerging societal expectations can lead to psychological distress. According to a report in the *American Psychological Association*, women facing the dual pressures of career and family responsibilities often experience heightened stress levels, which can lead to anxiety and depression (APA, 2017).

Biologically, women may also face unique health risks when taking on roles traditionally associated with men. For example, research has shown that women in high-stress jobs historically held by men have a higher risk of cardiovascular diseases compared to those in more traditional female roles (Kuper et al., 2002, *Journal of Epidemiology & Community Health*).

However, it is essential to note that these outcomes are not solely due to the roles themselves but rather the societal structures and supports, or lack thereof, surrounding these roles. The lack of adequate support systems, such as child-care and flexible work arrangements, exacerbates the stress associated with these non-traditional roles. Research in *The Lancet* highlights the importance of social support and work-life balance in mitigating the health risks related to role strain (Kivimäki et al., 2015).

In conclusion to what we just presented, while society's changing expectations of gender roles offer more opportunities for women, they also bring challenges that can impact physical and mental health. These challenges point to the need for societal changes supporting women in all roles they undertake.

However, there is a misunderstanding about the role of a father. Fathers are often considered the head of the household, but a more apt comparison is that of a foundation. A father should be viewed as the base that supports and stabilizes, much like a tree's roots or a house's foundation. This perspective emphasizes stability and support over dominance.

Embracing this concept means recognizing the critical role of a father, which we will discuss later in the next chapter. Educating men and young boys is essential, and being a father is not a role to be taken lightly or rushed into for short-term gratification. A father's position requires preparation and understanding; without these, relationships may suffer, and fathers may be overwhelmed by unexpected responsibilities.

The fairy tales and stories we see and hear often do not capture the reality of fatherhood. It is a significant, lifelong commitment that goes beyond the simplistic narratives usually portrayed in the media. Men should be encouraged to understand the depth of this commitment and to respect the process of becoming a father, recognizing the patience and dedication required to support and maintain a healthy family structure.

Being a father extends beyond seeking personal satisfaction or having someone to manage household chores. It involves the profound responsibility of caring for another human being. Clarifying this is crucial because many men feel underappreciated for their efforts at home.

However, men need to understand that fulfilling responsibilities such as paying bills, maintaining vehicles, and ensuring home safety are inherent duties of fatherhood. Seeking external praise for these actions is unnecessary. Instead, a father should find fulfillment in knowing his responsibilities are met and his family is well-cared for. Fathers should recognize that their role is to contribute to the household and nurture their family, not just receive acknowledgment for a completed task.

Reflecting on my journey into fatherhood, I recognize the void left by my father's absence. Growing up without a paternal figure meant I had to trek the roads of adolescence alone - from the changes in my body to understanding finances and relationships with women. This gap in guidance contributed to my struggles with weight as a child; I spent too much time indoors, passive, and not making the most of my youthful energy.

The common lamentation, "If only I knew then what I know now," resonates deeply with all of us. I often ponder how different my life might have been had I been armed with the wisdom and understanding I possess today. The advantages I could have gained from that knowledge and its application are immeasurable.

As a father, I am committed to being integral to my children's lives. I am diligent about their school work, household responsibilities, and extracurricular activities. Nevertheless, in my zeal, I sometimes catch myself pushing them too hard, driven by a desire to offer them the life I was denied. I have to remind myself that they are still children and that my role is to discipline them and provide them with the necessary knowledge to make informed decisions as they grow.

Recently, I reached out to my biological father and stepfather to express my yearning for their guidance during my formative years. Through this conversation, I discovered a cycle of unpreparedness; they also lacked role models. This revelation prompted me to reevaluate my feelings, and in doing so, I released any resentment I held. Like me, I realized they were doing their best with what they knew.

This epiphany has inspired me to lead a mission, with divine guidance, to break this cycle. I am determined to collaborate with other men to address this widespread lack of paternal advice. I want to cultivate a generation of well-informed fathers who understand their critical role in their children's lives and the fabric of the household.

THE ESSENCE OF FATHERHOOD: ROLES & RESPONSIBILITIES

In the preceding chapters, we have explored the multifaceted role of the father. In these brief descriptions, we go farther into the heart of fatherhood, illuminating the profound impact of paternal approval, the guiding light of purpose, and the enduring strength of responsibility. In addition, we intend to explore the future-oriented aspects of fatherhood, focusing on guiding the next generation toward their potential.

THE POWER OF PATERNAL APPROVAL

The quest for paternal approval is a common thread in the narrative of childhood and beyond. In his extensive research, Dr. Ronald P. Rohner of the University of Connecticut has highlighted the psychological benefits of parental acceptance and the detrimental impact of rejection. Rohner's studies suggest that paternal approval is a cornerstone of positive self-esteem and psychological well-being (Rohner, R. P., & Veneziano, R. A. (2001). "The importance of father love: History and contemporary evidence." Review of General Psychology, 5(4), 382-405). This resonates with my journey as a public speaker, where my stepfather's nod of recognition affirmed my path and imbued my endeavors with meaning and direction.

It is worth exploring how paternal approval's power influences various aspects of an individual's life. A father's approval, or lack thereof, can shape a person's identity, influence their career choices, and affect their relationships. Dr. Rohner's research underlines the immediate impact of paternal approval on self-esteem and psychological health and its long-term implications on social behavior and emotional stability.

Paternal approval often serves as a form of validation that children, even into adulthood, seek out. This validation can propel them towards specific achievements and can be a driving force behind their ambitions. Conversely, the absence of paternal approval can lead to a quest for validation elsewhere, sometimes in unproductive or unhealthy ways. The desire for this approval is deeply embedded in the psyche, influencing decisions and shaping the trajectory of one's life.

Moreover, paternal approval can enhance the resilience of individuals, equipping them to handle life's challenges with greater confidence. It contributes to a foundational sense of security and belonging, which is crucial for healthy psychological development. The impact of paternal approval—or its absence—extends beyond the individual, affecting societal structures and norms. It plays a role in perpetuating specific familial and social patterns, influencing how future generations conceptualize and enact fatherhood.

Incorporating this understanding into the broader conversation about fatherhood and its significance can enrich societal appreciation for fathers' subtle role. It can also inform support systems and interventions to foster positive family dynamics. Recognizing the profound impact of paternal approval and addressing its complexities can lead to more supportive environments that nurture healthy psychological development and well-being for all family members.

INSTILLING PURPOSE

A father's role extends to instilling a sense of purpose in his children. Dr. Kevin Washington, a psychologist and past president of the Association of Black Psychologists, articulates the importance of purpose relating to African-American youth and cultural identity. When a father imparts values and sense, he equips his child to navigate life's moral complexities with a clear internal compass (Washington, K. (2016). "The role of the Black father in the transmission of historical memory and cultural identity: A psycho-cultural approach to the healing of African American boys." Journal of Black Psychology, 42(1), 24-46).

Expanding on the concept of instilling purpose, a father's influence in imparting a sense of identity and moral direction is profound. This role is especially pivotal in communities where cultural identity and history are crucial in individual development and societal interaction. Dr. Kevin Washington's work emphasizes the critical function of African-American fathers in passing down cultural heritage and historical memory, serving as a vital link to past generations and as a guide for navigating present and future challenges.

This process of instilling purpose goes beyond simply teaching right from wrong; it involves embedding children with a sense of their history, culture, and unique place in the world. It's about fostering resilience through understanding one's roots and a deep-seated belief in one's capacity to effect change. For many African-American youths, this connection to cultural identity with historical context is a source of strength and empowerment in the face of systemic challenges and societal obstacles.

Moreover, the act of instilling purpose is intertwined with the development of a child's self-esteem and self-efficacy. When fathers actively engage in their children's lives by sharing stories of resilience, achievement, and perseverance from their cultural history, they educate them about their heritage and instill a sense of pride and a belief in their potential. This can be particularly empowering for children navigating environments where they may face racial and economic disparities.

By modeling behaviors and attitudes grounded in a strong cultural and moral framework, fathers teach their children how to respectfully, productively, and assertively interact with the broader society. They play a crucial role in preparing their children to confront and overcome discrimination and prejudice, equipping them with the tools to advocate for themselves and their communities.

In addition to fostering a connection to cultural identity, fathers who instill a sense of purpose in their children help them develop a personal vision for their future. This includes guiding them in setting goals, understanding their passions and talents, and encouraging them to contribute to their community and society. Such guidance helps children develop a clear sense of direction and an understanding of how they can achieve their aspirations.

In conclusion, a father's role in instilling purpose is indispensable. He is a foundational pillar in developing a child's identity, moral compass, and sense of belonging. This purposeful engagement supports children's psychological and emotional development and strengthens the social fabric by fostering confident, culturally connected, and morally grounded individuals. Dr. Washington's research underscores the transformative power of purposeful fatherhood in shaping the lives of African-American youth, offering insights that are universally applicable across all cultures and communities.

SHAPING THE FUTURE

A father plays a critical role in preparing his child for the future. According to a study by Dr. Sara S. McLanahan, children with involved fathers are more likely to achieve academic and career success (McLanahan, S., Tach, L., & Schneider, D. (2013). "The causal effects of father absence." Annual Review of Sociology, 399-427). This has been my narrative; without a clear direction from my father, I found myself adrift, highlighting the necessity for paternal guidance in forging a clear and focused future.

Fathers play a vital role in shaping their children's futures, and it's essential to delve deeper into the mechanisms through which paternal involvement influences children's long-term outcomes. Dr. Sara S. McLanahan's study underscores the significance of a father's presence in promoting academic and career achievements. Still, the impact extends beyond these areas, influencing social skills, emotional intelligence, and resilience against adversity.

Emotional and Social Development

Fathers contribute uniquely to their children's emotional and social development. Their interactions often encourage risk-taking, problem-solving, and independence, fostering a sense of confidence and self-reliance. How a father approaches life's challenges, resolves conflicts, and navigates his relationships serves as a model for his children, offering them a blueprint for interacting with the world around them.

Moral and Ethical Guidance

Moreover, fathers play a crucial role in their children's moral and ethical development. Through their actions and decisions, fathers impart values that become their children's moral compass. This guidance is crucial in helping children differentiate right from wrong and develop integrity, empathy, and compassion. The values instilled by a present and engaged father can guide children through life's ethical dilemmas and challenges.

Resilience and Coping Skills

a father's involvement also contributes significantly to a child's resilience. Fathers who support their children through failures and challenges while celebrating their successes help build a resilient psychological foundation to life's ups and downs. This resilience is critical for mental health and well-being, enabling children to confidently bounce back from setbacks and pursue their goals.

Career Aspirations and Achievement

Fathers influence their children's career aspirations and achievements through direct advice and the example they set in their professional lives. Children observe and often seek to emulate or exceed their father's accomplishments, finding inspiration in their father's work ethic, professional success, and passions. This can motivate children to set high aspirations and work diligently towards their goals.

In conclusion, the role of a father in shaping a child's future impacts not just academic and career success but also emotional and social development, moral guidance, and resilience. As highlighted by personal narratives, the absence of such paternal influence can leave a void that might lead individuals to feel adrift. Therefore, fostering environments where fathers are encouraged and supported to play active roles in their children's lives is essential for the well-being and future success of the next generation. Encouragingly, recognizing the critical role of fathers invites strategies and policies that support paternal involvement in all its forms, ultimately benefiting families and society as a whole.

CULTURAL HERITAGE AND CONFIDENCE

Moreover, fathers are custodians of heritage and tradition, which provide a sense of belonging and identity. As I reflect on my upbringing in a church-going family, the values and teachings of my father and grandfather kept me grounded. The psychologist Dr. Wade W. Nobles has emphasized the importance of cultural legacy in developing a positive identity in African American families (Nobles, W. W. (1974). "African philosophy: Foundations for Black psychology." In R. L. Jones (Ed.), Black Psychology (pp. 18-32). Harper & Row).

Fathers play a pivotal role in bridging past and future, embedding cultural values and traditions fundamental to their children's identity and self-perception. This crucial task ensures the transmission of customs, beliefs, and historical narratives across generations, enabling fathers to serve as living conduits of their heritage. Through storytelling and daily practices, they offer their children a rich identity tapestry, fostering a sense of pride and belonging that counters negative societal stereotypes and biases.

Drawing from the work of Dr. Wade W. Nobles, particularly his emphasis on the importance of cultural legacy and the African philosophy of Ubuntu—"I am because we are"—fathers can ground their children in a lineage that affirms their place in the world. This grounding is especially vital in communities like African Americans", where preserving cultural identity is both a challenge and an act of resilience. By nurturing a strong sense of cultural pride and belonging, fathers equip their children with the confidence to navigate societal challenges, instilling values of respect, resilience, and community service.

The impartation of cultural wisdom goes beyond mere education; it's about endowing children with the confidence to face the world, aware of their roots and the legacy they carry forward. Fathers shape their children's present and future self-conception by teaching about the past, ensuring they move through the world with an assured sense of self. This role as custodians of culture and identity transcends the boundaries of individual families, affecting the broader social fabric.

Fathers ensure the continuity of heritage and the nurturing of future generations by actively engaging in their children's cultural education. They teach their children to balance their cultural heritage with contemporary global influences, thus developing a powerful sense of self. This guidance is invaluable, providing children with a foundation of identity and values that empower them to contribute positively to their communities and the world. Through the legacy of those who came before them, children are inspired to build their dreams and feel secure in knowing who they are.

BUILDING CONFIDENCE AND SELF-EFFICACY

Contrary to the notion that only mothers play a pivotal role in nurturing confidence, the influence of fathers on their children's self-assurance is profound and significant. Dr. Joseph White, a trailblazer in Black psychology, underscored the critical role fathers play as role models in bolstering a child's confidence through both encouragement and the sharing of experiences traditionally seen as masculine (White, J. L. (1970). "Toward a Black Psychology." Ebony, 25(10), 44-48). This insight sheds light on fathers' indispensable impact on their children's development of self-confidence and identity.

Fathers uniquely contribute to their children's growth into confident individuals through their interactions, embodying what it means to approach life's hurdles with courage and integrity. These moments, especially those shared experiences that might align with traditional masculine activities, transcend gendered expectations, offering valuable lessons in resilience, curiosity, and perseverance. Whether engaging in sports, exploring nature, or intellectual discussions, fathers and children find common ground ripe for building confidence.

Fathers are more than just role models. They affirm their children's potential and skills. This affirmation is a powerful act of recognizing and valuing the child's abilities, laying the groundwork for a robust self-belief system. When a father expresses belief in his child's capabilities, he boosts the child's confidence. He instills resilience that empowers the child to face challenges head-on, nurturing a solid sense of self-efficacy.

Dr. White's perspective on the father's role also invites a broader societal reflection on fatherhood and masculinity. He challenges existing stereotypes and advocates for a more inclusive understanding of masculine identity that embraces empathy, vulnerability, and active participation in nurturing. This expanded narrative of fatherhood enhances the child's emotional and psychological development and enriches the paternal bond, offering a more comprehensive model of personal growth for the child.

Embracing Dr. White's insights into fatherhood means advocating for a parenting approach that values and promotes fathers' engagement in their children's lives, both emotionally and psychologically. It highlights the necessity of dismantling outdated views of paternal roles, encouraging a partnership in parenting that leverages the unique strengths and perspectives of both fathers and mothers. By championing the varied contributions of fathers to their children's sense of confidence and resilience, society can foster more nuanced and effective strategies for child-rearing that recognize the importance of diverse examples of strength and confidence for the benefit of all children.

FAMILY DYNAMICS AND RESPECT

Respect within the family dynamic is a value that fathers are uniquely positioned to teach. A father must impart to his children the principles of respect and decorum as they navigate the broader social world. This is echoed by Dr. Michael Eric Dyson, who speaks to the reverence for elders in African American culture as a cornerstone of familial respect (Dyson, M. E. (2005). "Is Bill Cosby right?: Or has the Black middle class lost its mind?". Basic Civitas Books).

A brief elaboration on Family Dynamics and Respect: it is essential to delve deeper into a father's role in embedding the value of respect within the fabric of family life. As taught by fathers, respect encompasses not only the reverence for elders, as highlighted by Dr. Michael Eric Dyson, but also a broader spectrum of interpersonal ethics, including empathy, understanding, and recognizing individual boundaries. Fathers can instill a profound knowledge of respect children carry into adulthood through their interactions, discipline, and the examples they set.

Respect within the family dynamic also involves teaching children how to engage with differing opinions, resolve conflicts constructively, and appreciate diversity in all its forms. These lessons, in respect, become foundational elements of a child's character, influencing their social interactions and shaping their approach to the world around them. Furthermore, fathers can demonstrate respect in treating the children's mother and other family members, providing a living model of respectful behavior for their children to emulate.

As Dr. Dyson suggests, respect is deeply tied to cultural norms and values. Thus, the teaching of respect can vary significantly from one cultural context to another. In many cultures, respect is closely linked to familial hierarchies and obligations, while in others, it may be more closely associated with mutual reciprocity and the acknowledgment of individuality within the family unit. Fathers, therefore, must navigate the cultural expectations surrounding respect while adapting these lessons to the evolving social norms of a globalized society.

Moreover, the digital age introduces new dimensions of respecting teaching. Fathers need to guide their children in navigating online interactions respectfully and safely. This includes helping them understand digital etiquette, the importance of privacy, and the impact of their digital footprint.

In conclusion, the role of fathers in teaching respect within the family dynamic is a critical aspect of parenting that has far-reaching implications for society. Fathers lay the groundwork for the next generation's social behavior and interpersonal relationships by imparting respect, etiquette, and empathy. This instruction in respect is about adherence to social norms and fostering a deep-seated sense of responsibility towards oneself and others. Through these lessons, fathers contribute to building a more respectful, understanding, and cohesive society.

CO-PARENTING WITH RESPECT

Even in the complexities of co-parenting, a father's responsibility extends to maintaining respect for the child's mother. Research by Dr. Linda Nielsen of Wake Forest University shows that children benefit from observing respectful co-parenting, regardless of the relationship status between parents (Nielsen, L. (2011). "Shared parenting after divorce: A review of shared residential parenting research." Journal of Divorce & Remarriage, 52(8), 586-609).

Co-Parenting with Respect, examining the significance of maintaining a respectful and collaborative co-parenting relationship, especially from a father's perspective. Dr. Linda Nielsen's research underscores the importance of shared parenting and its positive outcomes on children's well-being. This shared parenting approach emphasizes that both parents, regardless of their relationship with each other, have vital roles to play in their child's life.

Respectful co-parenting involves open communication, mutual Respect, and the ability to make joint decisions about the child's upbringing. It requires setting aside personal differences to prioritize the child's needs and well-being. Children who witness their parents interacting respectfully and co-operatively learn valuable communication, problem-solving, and emotional regulation lessons. They are more likely to feel secure and stable, knowing they are both parents' priority.

Moreover, respectful co-parenting sets a positive example of interpersonal relationships for children. It teaches them about Respect, empathy, and understanding in relationships, which are crucial skills for their social development. Children who grow up seeing their parents cooperate are more likely to develop healthy relationship patterns themselves.

It's also worth noting that respectful co-parenting contributes to a more amicable family environment, reducing the potential stress and conflict children might experience after parental separation. This can mitigate the negative impacts often associated with divorce or separation, such as emotional distress and behavioral issues.

In practice, respectful co-parenting can involve:

- Regular and clear communication about the child's needs.

- Sharing responsibilities equally.

- Supporting each other's relationship with the child.

It also means presenting a united front on parenting decisions and respecting each other's parenting styles and boundaries.

Ultimately, co-parenting with Respect is not just about the relationship between the child and each parent; it's about fostering a family dynamic that supports the child's overall development and happiness. Fathers play a crucial role in ensuring the co-parenting relationship is built on Respect, collaboration, and mutual support.

WORK ETHICS AND MORAL STANDARDS

The value of hard work is yet another critical teaching. Sociologist Dr. Elijah Anderson has discussed the "code of the street" and the contrasting "decent" father figures who instill the ethics of hard work and responsibility in their children (Anderson, E. (1999). "Code of the Street: Decency, Violence, and the Moral Life of the Inner City." W. W. Norton & Company

Fathers' teachings of work ethics and moral standards are pivotal, particularly in challenging environments. Dr. Elijah Anderson's exploration into the "code of the street" versus the "decent" father figures delineates a critical societal dichotomy. Fathers who embody and instill the ethics of hard work and responsibility serve as beacons of guidance, steering their children away from the adversities and moral pitfalls that can dominate their surroundings. Through their actions and expectations, these fathers demonstrate that maintaining a strong moral compass and a commitment to hard work is invaluable despite external pressures or societal expectations.

The influence of such father figures extends beyond immediate family dynamics, impacting the broader community. By setting examples of integrity, perseverance, and responsibility, these fathers lay the groundwork for their children to aspire to personal success and contribute positively to society. As Anderson describes, the lessons imparted by "decent" fathers encompass more than just the importance of hard work; they also include cultivating respect for oneself and others, the value of education, and the significance of making constructive choices.

Moreover, the contrast between the "code of the street" and the principles taught by these fathers highlights the role of parental guidance in navigating social identities and expectations. Fathers prioritizing work ethics and moral standards help their children discern right from wrong in complex social landscapes, empowering them to pursue pathways leading to productive and fulfilling lives.

In essence, fathers' teachings of work ethics and moral standards, especially within the context of Dr. Anderson's work, underscore the profound impact of paternal influence on children's moral and ethical development. These lessons shape the character and choices of the next generation and potentially transform the moral fabric of communities, fostering environments where decency, hard work, and responsibility are valued and replicated.

FATHERS AND THE FUTURE OF APPROVAL

As we look ahead, it becomes increasingly clear that a father's approval will continue to be a driving force in a child's development. Dr. Ronald P. Rohner's research will remain relevant, as future fathers will need to understand the depth of their influence on their child's self-esteem and life satisfaction.

The evolving dynamics of fatherhood and the quest for paternal approval highlight a crucial aspect of child development that extends into the fabric of future societal structures. As we navigate the changing landscapes of family life, influenced by shifts in cultural norms, technological advancements, and a deeper understanding of psychological health, the role of fathers and their approval takes on new dimensions.

Dr. Ronald P. Rohner's work lays a foundational understanding of fathers' significant impact on their children's psychological well-being. This understanding becomes a critical guidepost for future fathers, emphasizing the importance of being present in their children's lives and actively affirming their worth and achievements. The nuanced nature of paternal approval—emotional support, verbal affirmation, and active participation in the child's life—underscores fathers' multifaceted role in shaping their children's futures.

Moreover, as society continues to challenge and redefine traditional gender roles, the expression and reception of paternal approval may also evolve. Future fathers may find themselves navigating a landscape where emotional openness and vulnerability become as valued in their role as strength and protection have been historically. This shift could foster deeper connections between fathers and children, with profound implications for future generations' emotional and social development.

Additionally, the increasing acknowledgment of diverse family structures, including single-parent families, blended families, and LGBTQ+ parenting, will expand the understanding and application of paternal approval. Fathers and figures must adapt to these diverse contexts, finding ways to provide approval and support that resonate with each child's unique circumstances and needs.

In this context, the future of paternal approval is not just about maintaining its importance but about expanding its expression and understanding its impact in broader, more inclusive ways. Dr. Rohner's research offers a valuable starting point for this exploration, highlighting the enduring need for fathers to engage positively with their children. As we move forward, it will be essential for educational programs, parenting resources, and community support systems to incorporate these insights, empowering fathers to fulfill their pivotal role in their children's lives with awareness, sensitivity, and adaptability.

THE IMPARTING OF PURPOSE

Fathers of tomorrow will be expected to lay down a framework of purpose for their children. They will be tasked with helping their children navigate life's moral landscapes, echoing the principles highlighted by Dr. Kevin Washington. Fathers will provide a roadmap and enable their children to craft their paths grounded in a solid sense of self and cultural identity.

The role of fathers in imparting purpose to their children is increasingly recognized as pivotal in developing a child's sense of self and cultural identity. Dr. Kevin Washington, among others, has illuminated how the guidance fathers provide in navigating life's moral landscapes is instrumental in shaping individual character and societal values. As fathers of tomorrow face the challenge of preparing their children for an ever-evolving world, their role evolves beyond traditional expectations to include the nurturing of emotional intelligence, resilience, and adaptability.

In this context, the imparting of purpose involves more than setting a moral compass; it encompasses equipping children with the skills to evaluate, adapt, and thrive in diverse environments. Fathers are expected to model behaviors that reflect an understanding of global interconnectedness, demonstrating respect for different cultures and perspectives. This approach helps children develop a well-rounded cultural identity, fostering inclusivity and empathy.

Moreover, in laying down a framework of purpose, fathers must balance imparting cultural traditions with encouraging individuality. This delicate balance ensures that children appreciate their roots while feeling empowered to forge their unique paths. The ability to make informed choices, grounded in a strong sense of self and ethical principles, is a gift that fathers can provide, preparing their children for the complexities of modern life.

Furthermore, the digital age presents new challenges and opportunities in fatherhood. Fathers of tomorrow will guide their children through the digital landscape, teaching them to discern the vast amount of information and influence they encounter online. In doing so, fathers can help their children develop critical thinking and digital literacy, essential skills for the 21st century.

In summary, the imparting of purpose by fathers extends to fostering a robust and adaptable sense of self in their children, equipped to navigate both the digital world and the physical one with confidence and integrity. By providing a roadmap grounded in cultural identity and moral clarity, fathers contribute immeasurably to the personal development of their children and, by extension, to the shaping of a more compassionate and understanding society.

GUIDING TOWARDS ACHIEVEMENT

A father's responsibility in his child's educational and professional journey will be even more critical. Dr. Sara S. McLanahan's findings will be a cornerstone as fathers actively engage in their children's lives, enhancing their prospects for success. Fathers will aim to be both cheerleaders and advisors, encouraging exploration while providing the stability and focus needed to achieve long-term goals.

Fathers guiding their children towards achievement is essential to delve into the multifaceted role that fathers play in influencing their children's educational and professional journey. Dr. Sara S. McLanahan's research underscores the pivotal role of paternal involvement in boosting children's academic and career outcomes. This involvement ranges from educational support to developing soft skills necessary for success in life.

Fathers contribute uniquely to their children's development, complementing maternal influences with perspectives and support. Their involvement can manifest in various forms, from helping with homework to discussing career aspirations to modeling professional behavior and work ethic.

Such engagement not only aids in academic achievement but also cultivates a mindset geared toward lifelong learning and adaptability.

Moreover, fathers who actively participate in their children's education and career planning often instill in them a sense of responsibility, ambition, and confidence. They become role models for navigating challenges and setbacks, demonstrating resilience and problem-solving in real-world contexts. This guidance is crucial in preparing children for the complexities of the modern workplace and society.

Beyond the practical aspects of guidance, fathers provide invaluable emotional support. Encouragement boosts self-esteem and motivation, making children more likely to take on and persevere through challenging tasks. This emotional backing is especially significant in moments of doubt or fail-ure, helping children view these experiences as opportunities for growth rather than insurmountable obstacles.

A father's involvement in his child's educational and pro-fessional journey is a dynamic mix of mentorship, support, and modeling. As fathers aim to be both cheerleaders and advisors, their active engagement is vital to unlocking their children's potential and enhancing their prospects for suc-cess. Fathers' evolving role in this domain reflects a broader understanding of parenting as a partnership that profoundly impacts children's outcomes and achievements.

As we anticipate fatherhood's future, these themes will form the bedrock of fatherly duties. Fathers will be prepared to rise to the occasion, equipped with the wisdom of the past and the adaptability required for the ever-changing landscape of family dynamics.

THE MALE AND THE FAMILY

THE ESSENCE AND FOUNDATION OF THE FAMILY

Since the dawn of human civilization, the family has stood as the bedrock of society. It is the primal and most enduring institution, often hailed as the cure-all for social, spiritual, and national tribulations. Long before the advent of industrialization, with its factories and assembly lines, before the establishment of mills, processing plants, and educational systems, and even before the formation of armies and the unfolding of great scientific epiphanies, the concept of family was the nucleus of human existence. This is evident when one examines the matter through a spiritual or religious lens: At the beginning, there was a mother and a father, and from their union, children were born—a family was created.

The assertion that the family unit holds the salve for the plethora of societal, psychological, and emotional disorders of our past and present is not mere idealism. From the perspective of various religious and philosophical teachings, the family is not just a microcosm of society but a reflection of the order and harmony desired on a larger scale. Stoicism, for example, teaches the virtue of personal responsibility and the importance of roles within any group, particularly within the family. Seneca, a Stoic philosopher, once wrote, "The first bond of society is marriage; next, children; and then the family" (Seneca, "Moral Letters to Lucilius," Letter 87), highlighting the sequential importance of family relationships.

Moreover, Christian scriptures emphasize the sanctity of the family, with Paul the Apostle asserting in Ephesians 5:31-33 that the marital bond is sacred and reflective of the relationship between Christ and the Church. In Islam, the family is revered as a divine institution, with the Prophet Muhammad stating, "The best among you is the best to his family" (Hadith Tirmidhi), placing the family's welfare at the forefront of a Muslim's duties.

Similarly, Buddhism teaches the significance of familial bonds and responsibilities as a form of social harmony, as echoed in the Sigalovada Sutta, where the Buddha describes the mutual obligations between family members. Judaism, too, reveres the family unit, as seen in the Torah, where the commandment to "Honor your father and your mother" (Exodus 20:12) is one of the Ten Commandments. Thus, family is placed at the core of societal law and order.

Socially and historically, the family has been a critical element in community survival and prosperity. The family is a child's first school, where values, culture, and traditions are imparted, and emotional bonds are forged. Sociological research has consistently demonstrated the family's role in developing emotional stability and cultivating productive citizens. According to the American Psychological Association, secure family attachments are linked to healthier behavior patterns and better social outcomes (American Psychological Association, "Family and Relationships," 2012).

In the grander scope of national and international affairs, the principles of family—unity, cooperation, nurturing, and mutual respect—can offer insights into conflict resolution and governance. If nations interacted with the compassion and compromise expected within a healthy family, many of the world's conflicts could be approached with greater empathy and understanding.

The family, with its deep-seated roots in psychological well-being, historical continuity, and sociological health, is foundational to the individual and a model for the community, nation, and the international arena. To overlook its potential is to neglect the essence of human structure and societal order. As we navigate the complexities of the modern world, it is in the simplicity and enduring strength of the family unit that we may find the wisdom and solutions for a harmonious future.

- Historically and across cultures, the family is the primary unit for reproduction and nurturing; through this lens, we can understand its profound importance. As the eminent sociologist David Popenoe argues, "The family is the nucleus of civilization and the basic social unit of society" (Popenoe, 1993). It is in the family where the first and most critical stages of human development occur. Psychologist Urie Bronfenbrenner's ecological systems theory underscores this, showing how the microsystem of the family impacts individual development (Bronfenbrenner, 1979).

· It is not an overstatement to consider the family as the prototype of society; it is where individuals learn to communicate, cooperate, and coexist. The skills and values imparted within the family unit—empathy, trust, and mutual support—are the building blocks of societal structure. In his 1947 book "Family and Civilization," Harvard sociologist Carle Zimmerman traced societies' rise and fall and found a strong correlation with the health of family life.

· Moreover, the strength of a society can often be directly traced to the health of its family units. The family's role in providing emotional security and social stability has been documented extensively. Sociologist James Q. Wilson wrote about families' fundamental role in socializing children and providing social and moral order (Wilson, 1985).

· The reflection of society's conditions in the family unit is stark. Sociological research has shown that when families are under stress, this is mirrored in society through increased social problems like crime and poverty (Sampson et al., 1997). Conversely, robust and supportive family structures contribute to a more resilient and cohesive community.

· The security provided by families is more than just emotional; it is a bulwark against societal disintegration. The sanctity of the family is indeed the bedrock of human survival, and a sentiment echoed in the Universal Declaration of Human Rights, which states that the family is "the natural and fundamental group unit of society and is entitled to protection by society and the State" (United Nations, 1948).

· Historically, families have predated formal government structures, and in many ways, they have laid the groundwork for governance. Political scientists like Robert Putnam have discussed how the bonds formed within family units spill over into civic engagement and democratic stability (Putnam, 2000).

· The abolishment of the family can lead to society's dissolution. When the family structure erodes, social structures are often quick to follow, as seen in the historical examinations of civilizations by historians like Arnold Toynbee, who studied the rise and fall of 21 civilizations and noted the importance of strong family bonds in the prosperity of societies.

· Lastly, while the state is interested in the welfare of families, it is crucial to recognize the limits of governmental intervention in the familial sphere. As a pre-state institution, the family has sovereign dynamics that should be respected. This idea is supported by the principle of subsidiarity, which is upheld in the social doctrine of the Catholic Church, indicating that matters ought to be handled by the smallest, lowest, or least centralized competent authority (Pontifical Council for Justice and Peace, 2004).

In summary, the principles revolving around the family as the foundation of society are deeply rooted in psychological, historical, and sociological evidence. The family's role in shaping individuals and, by extension, societies is irrefutable. Its preservation is essential for the continuity and health of civilization itself.

MODERN ALCHEMY OF MANHOOD

REFINING IDENTITY IN THE 21ST CENTURY

Imagine being asked to do something utterly new, interpreted differently by every individual based on their unique beliefs and cultural backgrounds. Think of being requested to carry out a task that requires a specific tool or technique you're unfamiliar with, with no training or guidance to light your way. Tough to do, right? In that case, you can begin to empathize with the complex journey of a boy transitioning into manhood. This journey is troubled with many contradictory expectations shaped by society, gender norms, unstable communities, and religious and educational institutions. Young men are silently grappling with these norms while also being stung by cultural double standards, the hydra-headed beast that demands from them an impossible perfection.

Men are often expected to be leaders who are strict yet not oppressive, competitive and dominant yet fair and relentless without showing any sign of weakness. They are pressured to know how to handle every situation, often needing to understand the rationale or the methods involved. The call to "be a real man," a vague and constantly evolving idea, can be a weighty challenge.

For generations, the definition of manhood has been in flux, its codes and roles changing with the cultural tides. In modern society, many traditional masculine traits are now viewed as outdated, and the rapid changes in what is considered "men's work" add to the confusion. As we evolve, our roles as protectors and providers have shifted from literal hunting and gathering to navigating digital marketplaces and enjoying leisurely pursuits like fishing as a sport rather than a necessity.

Technological advancements have transformed trades such as construction into industries where 3D printing and drones play a significant part, hinting at a future where automation and robotics dominate. Meanwhile, security measures have advanced so far that surveillance systems and personal gadgets now fill the once-critical role of the vigilant warrior.

As we face these seismic shifts in roles and expectations, men are often left wondering what their place is in a world where their traditional roles are becoming less recognized or needed. Manhood is being redefined, not just by societal standards but also by the emergence of gender politics, inclusivity, and the questioning of historical gender norms.

Yet, amid these changes, the core challenges of manhood persist. Some men may retreat when adversity strikes, while others might lose their drive to challenge the status quo. Mentalities will vary widely, from defeatism to proactive optimism. As society embraces a broader spectrum of gender identities, including the celebration of homosexuality and the softening of traditional masculine traits, it begs the question of what being a man truly entails today.

This identity crisis is a reflective struggle for men and bears profound implications for guiding the next generation. With an increasing number of boys growing up in single-parent households, the call to "man up" becomes an empty echo if the very models of manhood are absent or unclear.

The conversations that dominate our era often center on gender roles and relationships, yet they barely scratch the surface of these deeper issues. Amidst debates about value and respect, men's fundamental questions of identity and purpose still need to be addressed, creating a vacuum where the rules of manhood are no longer clear. This is especially true in a landscape where some modern societal movements quickly label traditional viewpoints outdated or offensive.

Therefore, the quintessential question we must confront is not just about defining manhood in the 21st Century but also about understanding what it means to be a man today—beyond the shadows cast by stereotypes and cultural archetypes. Only by doing so can we hope to provide a sense of direction and identity to those navigating the intricate voyage from boyhood to manhood.

In addressing the quintessential question of what it means to be a man today, the preferred perspective would consider the harmonization of self-mastery, responsibility, and community engagement as pillars upon which a modern definition of manhood can rest. Through self-mastery, a man cultivates the virtues of discipline and resilience, not merely to stand firm against life's adversities but to forge character in the crucible of his challenges. This inner governance is the bedrock for responsible action, where a man provides for himself and his loved ones and contributes to the well-being of those around him. He's a responsible man who recognizes his role as a steward, taking accountability for his successes and failures, learning, and teaching through them.

The essence of community engagement then builds upon these personal virtues, channeling them outward. Here, the concepts of leadership and legacy come to the forefront—where being a man entails being a pillar for others to lean on, a source of wisdom and strength. In the community, a man's actions speak to cultivating an environment where the young can grow, the peers can cooperate, and the elders are respected. In the community, the man's role as a mentor and example becomes fully realized, showcasing that manhood is not a static state of being but an active and dynamic contribution to society.

The modern man, therefore, recognizes the power of his individuality but also understands the strength of his connection to others. He is both a fortress and a bridge—solid in his convictions yet open to the wisdom of collective human experience. In the continuum of manhood, he learns, adapts, and evolves, understanding that the masculinity of the past does not need to be discarded but can be refined and redefined in the context of present realities and future aspirations. The answers to what it means to be a man are possibly innumerable, reflecting the diversity of roles men play and their diverse paths. Yet, they converge on these universal themes of self-control, accountability, and societal contribution, which stand as testaments to the enduring spirit of manhood.

The Evolution of Masculinity: From Past to Present

Few concepts in the ever-evolving human society have transformed as dramatically as masculinity. From the rigid, stoic figures of history to the more emotionally intelligent and adaptable men of today, masculinity has been redefined in ways that both challenge and complement traditional ideals. We want to explore this transformation and offer insights for men trying to helm these changes and for a broader audience, including high school and college students and women, who play a crucial role in shaping and understanding these evolving dynamics.

The Traditional Model of Masculinity

Traditionally, masculinity was synonymous with strength, both physical and emotional. Men were the unyielding pillars of society – stoic, resilient, and decisive. They were providers and protectors, roles rooted in physical prowess and emotional fortitude. This model of masculinity emphasized values like honor, duty, and responsibility, which are still admirable and relevant today.

However, this model also had its limitations. Emotional expression was often seen as a weakness, leaving little room for men to discuss feelings of fear, sadness, or vulnerability openly. This repression, while exalting the image of the 'strong, silent type,' often led to isolation and unaddressed mental health issues.

The Shift in the 21st Century

As society entered the 21st Century, the traditional model of masculinity began to shift. This change was propelled by increased gender equality, greater awareness of mental health, and a broader acceptance of diverse emotional expressions. Today's masculinity values emotional intelligence and vulnerability as strengths. Men are encouraged to communicate openly and honestly, show empathy, and actively participate in their mental and emotional well-being.

Modern masculinity also embraces flexibility and adaptability. In a rapidly changing world, men often must balance multiple roles – as caregivers, partners, and professionals. This Shift from the traditional, usually singular role of the 'provider' allows for a more holistic and fulfilling personal and professional life.

Understanding the Impact on Women and Society

This evolution in masculinity is not just a men's issue. It has profound implications for women and society at large. As masculinity becomes more emotionally intelligent and adaptable, relationships become more equitable and nurturing. Women, who have long shouldered the emotional labor in personal and professional spaces, find more allies and partners in men who embrace these modern ideals.

Moreover, this Shift challenges harmful stereotypes and social norms, creating a more inclusive and diverse understanding of gender roles. It opens up opportunities for everyone, regardless of gender, to explore and express their strengths and vulnerabilities without the constraints of traditional gender expectations.

The journey of masculinity from the past to the present is not just about redefining what it means to be a man. It's about creating a more compassionate, empathetic, and adaptable society. As we embrace the positive aspects of both traditional and modern masculinity, we pave the way for a future where emotional intelligence, respect, and equality are ideals and lived realities. This evolution benefits everyone, creating a world where each individual can thrive, unencumbered by outdated notions of what it means to be masculine or feminine. For high school and college students, and indeed for all of us, understanding and supporting this transformation in masculinity is vital to building a more inclusive and harmonious world.

What does that look like?

It is fascinating and compounded to create a way for a man to refine his identity using historical and modern ideologies of masculinity. It involves understanding the evolution of masculinity over time and integrating aspects that are healthy, positive, and relevant to the contemporary context. Here's a guide that blends historical and modern views:

UNDERSTANDING HISTORICAL MASCULINITIES

Stoicism and Emotional Control: Traditionally, men were expected to be stoic and control their emotions. This doesn't mean suppressing emotions but understanding and managing them effectively.

Responsibility and Duty: Historical masculinity emphasized responsibility, be it in the family, community, or battlefield. This sense of duty can be a powerful motivator and anchor in modern life.

Physical Strength and Resilience: The traditional view of masculinity often included physical prowess. Today, this can translate into caring for one's physical health and resilience, not necessarily for dominance but for well-being.

Honor and Integrity: These timeless values have always been central to traditional masculinity, focusing on living a life of integrity and honor.

INTEGRATING MODERN PERSPECTIVES

Emotional Intelligence and Vulnerability: Modern masculinity embraces the understanding that being emotionally intelligent and occasionally vulnerable is a strength, not a weakness. This contrasts with traditional views but is crucial for mental health and genuine relationships.

Equality and Respect for All: Contemporary masculinity includes respecting all genders and embracing equality, a departure from historical norms where men were often seen as dominant.

Self-Improvement and Lifelong Learning: The modern man understands the value of continuous learning and self-improvement in all aspects of life, including emotional, intellectual, and physical.

Balance and Flexibility: Modern life often demands a balance between work, personal life, and mental health. The modern man strives for this balance and adapts to changing roles in family and society.

PRACTICAL STEPS FOR REFINING IDENTITY

Self-Reflection: Regularly reflect on personal values, emotions, and goals. This can include journaling, meditation, or therapy.

Education and Learning: Stay informed about historical and modern views of masculinity. Read books, attend workshops, and engage in conversations that challenge and expand your understanding.

Physical Health: Maintain a healthy lifestyle that includes exercise, a balanced diet, and adequate sleep, reflecting the historical value of physical strength.

Emotional Health: Develop emotional intelligence through mindfulness, therapy, or open peer conversations.

Building Relationships: Focus on building meaningful and respectful relationships in all spheres of life.

Community Involvement: Engage in community service or group activities that foster a sense of responsibility and connection.

Adaptability: Be open to change and adaptable to new roles and ideas, balancing traditional and modern expectations.

Ethical living means living a life that aligns with one's values of integrity and honor and staying true to moral principles in all decisions.

Refining masculinity is a personal journey that involves balancing traditional values with modern understanding. It's about embracing the best aspects of both worlds—being strong yet emotionally intelligent, responsible yet flexible, and independent yet empathetic. This journey is not about fitting into a prescribed mold but creating an authentic, balanced, and respectful identity in today's diverse and ever-changing world.

DECIPHERING MARITAL PATTERNS: A SCIENTIFIC GLIMPSE INTO MODERN RELATIONSHIP DYNAMICS

There is a strong reason supported by the sciences that educate us on why the fabric of societal relationships is undergoing a dramatic transformation. Recent statistics that show 44% of marriages end in divorce, 33% of adult men never marry, and 19% are separated provide a stark representation of modern relational trends. This chapter adds more understanding to the scientific reasons behind these significant figures, exploring how societal, psychological, and economic factors intertwine to shape these contemporary marital outcomes. And we believe this information is needed.

SOCIETAL EVOLUTION AND MARITAL DECISIONS

The decision to marry, separate, or stay single no longer follows a monolithic pattern, as was seen in traditional societies. Sociologists attribute the decline in marriage rates to a paradigm shift in societal norms and expectations. The cultural script that once directed people to marry as a rite of passage has been rewritten by newer generations prioritizing individual fulfillment and personal growth over societal expectations. The rise of gender equality movements has also played a significant role, as women, in particular, have more autonomy and economic independence than in the past, reducing the necessity of marriage for financial security.

ECONOMIC FACTORS AND MARITAL VIABILITY

Economic stability is a cornerstone of marital success. The sciences of economics and sociology collectively affirm that financial strain can lead to marital discord and, eventually, separation or divorce. Conversely, the decision to not marry can also be economically driven. With the increase in the cost of living and the burden of debt, especially among younger adults, economic pressures can delay or discourage marriage. In some cases, pursuing higher education and career advancement can further contribute to the delay in marital commitments, as individuals prioritize financial stability over marital status.

PSYCHOLOGICAL PERSPECTIVES ON RELATIONSHIPS

Psychology offers profound insights into the rising divorce rates and the hesitancy to enter into marriage. The compatibility of attachment styles, communication skills, and conflict resolution strategies are pivotal in determining the success of a marriage. Deviations in these areas can lead to dissatisfaction and eventual separation. Moreover, the modern emphasis on personal fulfillment can result in higher expectations for marriage, which, when unmet, may lead to disillusionment and a decision to divorce or remain unmarried.

THE INFLUENCE OF TECHNOLOGY AND SOCIAL CHANGE

Technology has revolutionized social interactions and, by extension, relationship dynamics. The constant connectivity and the paradox of choice presented by social media and dating platforms can create an environment where relationships are easily formed and just as quickly dissolved. Virtual space offers many options, making the commitment to one person a decision continuously under scrutiny and compared against potential alternatives.

The intersection of societal, economic, and psychological sciences provides a multidimensional understanding of the current marital landscape. It explains why a significant percentage of the population finds themselves divorced, separated, or never married. As the fabric of societal norms continues to evolve with changing economic conditions and technological advancements, so will the patterns of relationships. Policymakers, educators, and social scientists must understand these dynamics to support the well-being of individuals navigating the complexities of modern relationships.

ENGAGED FATHERHOOD: STRATEGIES FOR MAINTAINING VITAL CONNECTIONS WITH CHILDREN POST-DIVORCE OR SEPARATION

Maintaining a presence in their children's lives is a crucial aspect for fathers who are facing divorce separation or who have never married. Experts in psychology, family law, and social work often emphasize the importance of several key strategies to help fathers stay connected with their children.

First and foremost, it's essential to establish and maintain a positive co-parenting relationship. This means that fathers must work cooperatively with their children's other parents. According to Emery (2011), co-parenting requires that both parents set aside their grievances and focus on the well-being of the children. This includes regular communication about the children's needs, schedules, and meaningful life events. It also means showing mutual respect in front of the children to model positive conflict resolution and emotional maturity.

Legal avenues are also vital for protecting a father's right to be involved in his children's lives. Fathers should seek legal counsel to understand their rights and help negotiate parenting agreements or custody arrangements in the children's best interests. Wallerstein and Lewis (2004) stress the importance of such agreements as they provide a structured plan that ensures regular contact with the children.

Another crucial strategy involves staying emotionally engaged with the children. This includes being actively involved in their day-to-day lives, whether helping with homework, knowing their interests, attending school events, or being there for important milestones. Lamb (2010) suggests that the quality of the father-child relationship is more important than the quantity of time spent together. Thus, fathers should make the most of their time with their children, ensuring it is meaningful and nurturing.

Furthermore, experts recommend that fathers continue educating themselves about child development and parenting. By understanding the needs of their children at different stages, fathers can better support them emotionally and psychologically. This also shows the children that their father is committed to being integral to their lives.

Lastly, social support is critical. Fathers should seek out support groups or counseling if needed. The support can come from family, friends, or community groups, including those specifically tailored for single or divorced fathers. This support network can provide emotional support, practical advice, and sometimes just a listening ear.

In conclusion, staying involved in children's lives post-divorce or separation is a key factor for successful children. It involves fostering a cooperative co-parenting relationship, securing legal rights, being emotionally engaged, continuing parental education, and seeking social support. Each of these components helps to ensure that fathers remain a significant and positive influence in their children's lives, even when not in a traditional family setting.

FROM HER PERSPECTIVE

WE ARE EXPLORING THE ROLE OF FATHERS THROUGH THE LENS OF WOMEN.

According to a survey by the Pew Research Center, most women acknowledge the importance of fathers in child-rearing, emphasizing emotional support and discipline (Pew Research Center, 2021). In feminist perspectives, Gloria Steinem notably highlighted the transformative potential of fatherhood, stating, 'Fathers, like mothers, are not born. Men grow into fathers – and fathering is a critical stage in their development.' This reflects a broader understanding of fatherhood beyond traditional roles, emphasizing emotional engagement and active participation in domestic life. Studies further support this view, indicating that children with involved fathers experience better emotional, academic, and social outcomes (Journal of Family Psychology, 2020). These insights collectively underline the evolving narrative of fatherhood, championing a more engaged and nurturing role that transcends conventional boundaries and aligns with contemporary feminist thought.

The role of a father, as seen through the lenses of science, metaphysics, philosophy, esoteric traditions, and history, presents a rich and varied picture. Scientifically, the father's role is critical in the psychosocial development of children, with psychologists like John Bowlby and Michael E. Lamb underscoring the importance of emotional involvement and behavior modeling for a child's secure development. Metaphysically, fathers symbolize authority and structure, a concept echoed in Carl Jung's work (*pronounced with a hard K for his first name and 'Y-oong' for his surname, Jung*). Philosophically, thinkers like Aristotle have connected fatherhood with moral and intellectual formation. In esoteric and spiritual realms, the father figure is often sacred and symbolic, epitomized by the reverence commanded in many religious texts, such as the Biblical instruction to "Honor your father and your mother" (Exodus 20:12).

Historically, the perception and expectations of fatherhood have evolved dramatically. Ancient and medieval societies typically viewed fathers as the heads of families, responsible for protection, provision, and moral guidance. This view has shifted significantly, particularly after the Industrial Revolution, leading to a more emotionally connected and actively involved image of fatherhood in the modern era. This evolution reflects the broader societal changes in understanding the paternal role, suggesting, as anthropologist Margaret Mead aptly put it, "Fathers are biological necessities, but social accidents." This highlights the inherent biological function of fathers while acknowledging the diverse and ever-changing social constructs surrounding fatherhood, illustrating the dynamic and multifaceted nature of what it means to be a father.

Unraveling the Layers of Margaret Mead's Perception of Fatherhood

Forgive me, but we'll need to make a little detour. What she said was a little disturbing. I want to unpack that, gain more understanding, be logical, and not be emotionally disturbed. An eminent American cultural anthropologist, Margaret Mead has left an indelible mark on studying societal structures and human relationships. One of her most striking statements is that "fathers are biological necessities, but social accidents." We needed to analyze and understand the different meanings in this statement thoroughly and hopefully shed light on how it affects the worldview of fatherhood in biological and social-cultural terms.

Understanding the Biological Necessity

Firstly, Mead's reference to fathers as "biological necessities" acknowledges the fundamental role of men in the biological process of procreation. From a purely physical standpoint, the father's contribution of genetic material is indispensable for creating offspring. This aspect of fatherhood is rooted in the natural sciences. It is straightforward, emphasizing the father's role in continuing the human species. And that can't be done by either gender alone. It takes both of us. We don't mean to bore you with science and blah blah blah info you may care less about. However, when discussing specific topics, it is needed. And It's common sense to see that she's right in the first part of her statement. Because paternal genes not only influence specific traits and genetic predispositions in children, as indicated by research in the *American Journal of Human Genetics* but paternal health and lifestyle choices can also impact the epigenetic markers in sperm, affecting the long-term health of offspring, according to findings in the *International Journal of Epidemiology*.

Additionally, from an evolutionary biology perspective, fathers' role extends to investing in offspring, which is crucial for their development and survival. This investment, highlighted in evolutionary research, such as *Evolution and Human Behavior*, includes protection and resource provision, shaping human evolutionary strategies. Therefore, the father's role in the biological process of procreation is multifaceted, influencing the genetic makeup of the next generation and their development, health, and evolutionary success.

The Notion of Social Accidents

However, the phrase "social accidents" introduces a more complex and critical examination of fathers' role in society. Here, Mead suggests that the societal role and significance attributed to fathers are not inherent or essential but products of social constructs and historical circumstances. This implies that fathers' roles, responsibilities, and expectations could vary significantly across cultures and historical periods.

The traditional role of fathers as primary breadwinners is increasingly being reevaluated in today's society, where economic and social changes have significantly influenced family dynamics. Historically, men were often the primary earners, with job markets and societal norms during periods like the Industrial Revolution favoring male-dominated employment. These jobs typically demanded long hours or were located away from home, limiting men's involvement in everyday parenting.

However, as economies have evolved towards more service-oriented and knowledge-based sectors, and with the rise of gender equality movements, women have increasingly joined the workforce. This includes assuming roles in traditionally male-dominated fields, even those involving physical risk. Modern examples, like women working in construction and females enlisted taking on combat positions regarding their MOS or firefighting roles, challenge the long-standing norms of male and female responsibilities. Consequently, the economic need for fathers to be the sole breadwinners has lessened, opening doors for them to engage more actively in childcare and domestic life.

This shift in family roles has led to discussions around society's perceived emasculation and feminization. The term 'emasculation' reflects the challenge to traditional masculinity when men are no longer the sole financial providers, potentially causing feelings of insecurity. 'Effeminization' points to men adopting roles traditionally associated with women, like caregiving and nurturing, especially in dual-income households where sharing domestic responsibilities becomes essential.

However, it's crucial to understand that these shifts are not necessarily negative. The economic empowerment of women and the changing gender dynamics can be seen as an opportunity for a more equitable distribution of family responsibilities. This evolution allows roles to be based on individual strengths and preferences rather than being dictated by rigid gender norms. These changes reshape society, move away from traditional stereotypes, and pave the way for more balanced and diverse family structures.

We can argue that men's changing societal roles and perceptions do not diminish their importance or render them "social accidents," as Margaret Mead's statement suggests. Instead, these changes could be seen as broadening men's social and familial contributions beyond the traditional confines of being primary breadwinners.

The term "social accident" in Mead's statement implies a certain randomness or lack of necessity in fathers' social roles. However, they are driven by a deeper understanding of gender equality and the benefits of shared parenting responsibilities. Men's participation in traditionally seen feminine roles, such as nurturing and caregiving, doesn't make them accidents; instead, it highlights their adaptability and the malleability of social roles.

Furthermore, the value of fathers in a child's life extends beyond economic provision. Numerous studies have shown the positive impact of an engaged and present father on a child's emotional, social, and cognitive development. This influence is a testament to the fact that men are not merely 'biological necessities' but key players in the holistic development of their children.

To conclude, while Mead's statement captures the historical variability of the father's role, it only encompasses part of the scope of a father's significance in a family and society. Men are not 'social accidents' but integral parts of the social fabric, with roles that evolve in response to societal needs and values. The current trend towards more involved fatherhood reflects a broader understanding of the importance of men in family dynamics, challenging the notion that their roles are random or unnecessary. In modern society, men's contributions as breadwinners and caregivers are increasingly recognized as vital and valuable, solidifying their place as biological necessities and essential social pillars.

Cultural Variability and Historical Context

In some societies, fathers are seen as primary caregivers; in others, they are primarily breadwinners or even largely absent figures. In some cultures, fathers are primary caregivers, deeply involved in their children's nurturing and upbringing. This could include feeding, bathing, teaching, and playing with their children. An example of this can be seen in the Aka tribe in Central Africa, where fathers are often seen holding or staying near their children, actively participating in all aspects of childcare. These examples illustrate that the social role of fathers is not a fixed concept but one that is malleable and shaped by the cultural and historical context in which they live.

In conclusion, Margaret Mead's assertion that "fathers are biological necessities, but social accidents" is a multifaceted statement that touches on the core of anthropological inquiry into the nature of human relationships and societal structures. It acknowledges the undeniable biological role of fathers while simultaneously challenging the rigid, culturally constructed norms surrounding their social roles. Through this lens, Mead being respectfully disrespectful not only underscores the fluidity and variability of paternal roles across different societies but also encourages reevaluating the traditional perceptions of fatherhood, paving the way for a more inclusive and adaptable understanding of parental roles in the modern world.

Let's move on and get back on track.

THE ROLE OF A FATHER IS MORE THAN A PROVIDER

The role of a father extends far beyond the provision of financial stability; it is an amalgamation of mentorship, presence, and legacy. Current research underscores the profound impact a father's involvement has on their children's cognitive, social, and emotional development. According to a study by Howard, C. J., & Hill, N. E. in the "Journal of Negro Education," active fatherly presence is linked to better educational outcomes and fewer behavioral problems in African American children.

Contrastingly, a life spent in the relentless cycle of a detested job, in which a father invests hours into a company without ownership or personal fulfillment, sparks a debate on the actual cost of such labor. This traditional path often leaves fathers absent from pivotal moments of their children's lives —first words, first steps, first achievements. It begs the question: What legacy does such commitment leave behind?

In my experience, my stepfather's dedication to his role at Lockheed Martin, despite its high financial rewards and global travel opportunities, came at the cost of personal time that was rarely, if ever, taken. The value of such sacrifice is questionable, especially when attempts at nepotism in business reveal a harsh reality. My expectation of benefiting from my father's position was met with silence, a common scenario discussed in studies examining employment strategies in various communities. For instance, it is noted that in some cultures, children are expected to join the family business, accelerating their adulthood at the expense of their childhood (Smith, A. D., & Chowa, G. A. in "Children and Youth Services Review").

My reflections led me to consider alternative paternal roles exemplified by a friend, Travis, whose father, despite not being present for many life events, shared a passion for car mechanics with him. This shared interest in restoring a classic Mustang created a cherished and lasting bond. It exemplifies how fathers can connect with their children profoundly, even if traditional expressions of involvement are lacking.

In the African-American community, there is a significant emphasis on generational knowledge and skill transfer. As Michael A. Lindsey, Executive Director of the McSilver Institute for Poverty Policy and Research at NYU, articulates, "The legacy of knowledge and skills passed down from fathers is a measure of generational success" (Lindsey, M. A., "Journal of Black Studies"). Without such transfer, a father may become what could be considered a "generational failure," having missed the opportunity to enrich his family's lineage with his wisdom and expertise.

Ultimately, the father's role is to provide identity and direction for their children. Dr. Jawanza Kunjufu echoes this sentiment in his book Lessons From History: A Celebration in Blackness, emphasizing the father's role in shaping how the world recognizes children and, significantly, how they identify themselves.

As I ponder the unrealized experiences with my father, such as building a house together, I wonder about the missed opportunities for skill acquisition and bonding. It becomes clear that a father's legacy is not merely in the material or professional realm but profoundly seated in the shared experiences and teachings that equip the next generation with a career path and a life compass. A father's legacy is profoundly installed in these shared experiences and teachings. This encompasses more than the practical skills of hammering nails or managing finances; it's about imparting resilience, instilling values, and nurturing emotional intelligence.

Considering this profound role, a man can find his confidence and take pride in being a father. He must understand that his influence extends beyond the tangible into character-building and emotional development. He must embrace his strengths and vulnerabilities to improve in this role, recognizing that his journey is about leading and learning alongside his child.

Firstly, confidence in fatherhood comes from the understanding that a father's role is not to provide all the answers but to guide them in their quest. It's about demonstrating that life is a continuous journey of learning and growth. This approach fosters resilience in the child and reinforces the father's confidence in his crucial role as a guide, not an oracle.

Secondly, pride in fatherhood is nurtured by recognizing a father's unique contribution to his child's life. This isn't solely about financial provision or career guidance; it's about the emotional and moral compass a father provides. Every conversation, every shared experience, every display of vulnerability, and every moment of joy contribute to the child's understanding of the world and their place in it.

In concluding this chapter, it's essential to revisit the core message of our book: "To be one, he has to see one." A father's journey is an ever-evolving path marked by lifelong learning. He must embrace new experiences and adapt to the dynamic nature of the 21st century. He must be adaptable and resilient today, showing his children how to navigate the ever-changing world with grace and strength.

Effective communication stands as a cornerstone in this journey. It is about imparting wisdom and actively listening to the child's fears, hopes, and dreams. Deep, empathetic engagement strengthens the father-child bond and offers a window into the child's evolving world.

Equally important is the practice of empathy and patience. Seeing the world through a child's eyes, understanding their unique perspective, and guiding them with a patient hand truly defines fatherhood in its most profound sense. Patience is more than a virtue here; it's an essential tool as children grow and learn at their own unique pace.

As we close this chapter, let's reiterate the powerful notion that to be a father indeed, one must see the world through the lens of fatherhood – embracing lifelong learning, engaging in effective communication, and practicing empathy and patience. Let this be a call to action for all fathers and father figures: strive to embody these qualities, for in doing so, you enrich your own life and shape the future of the children who look up to you. Be the role model they need, the guide they seek, and the support they cherish. "To be one, he has to see one" – be that one and pave the way for a generation of empathetic, resilient, and well-guided individuals.

UNSEEN CURRENTS

THE IMPACT OF A FATHER'S ABSENCE

Regarding relationship patterns

In the journey through the complex landscape of relationships, we arrive at a crossroads where separation and divorce intersect. This chapter invites us to look beneath the surface of marital dissolution to explore the less discussed yet potent undercurrents contributing to the fragmentation of couples. While the usual suspects like infidelity, financial woes, and irreconcilable differences are known to all, it is the silent, pervasive cycles of trauma and instability that feed the roots of disunion. As reflections of society's broader familial dynamics, these profound issues deserve our attention and a place in the more general conversation on maintaining the integrity of intimate bonds. For single women, particularly those who have navigated life without a father's presence, understanding these patterns is crucial in recognizing and healing the past's hold on the present.

The decision to separate involves a complex interplay of factors and, statistically, is often initiated by men for various reasons. As we progress, this section should explain how fathers may inadvertently let down their daughters, which in turn influences boys, perpetuating a cycle where women may find themselves as single mothers—disconnected from the children's fathers for numerous reasons.

Growing up in the shadow of separation, these children might eventually perpetuate this familial pattern into their adult lives. We must confront and resolve these driving separation issues to break this cycle and fortify the family structure. What are these additional issues that are liable for breakups?

Some women have become too clingy

In family dynamics and relationship psychology, it is essential to recognize that childhood patterns often influence adult relationship behavior. In "To Be One He Has to See One: The Only Way a Boy Becomes a Righteous Man," we grapple with the complexities of how early parental interactions shape the maturation process.

If we look at the father archetype as sketched in various psychological theories, the presence and quality of fathering are instrumental in a child's development.

The father archetype represents authority, discipline, and the framework of societal norms. According to Jungian psychology, the absence of this paternal archetype can lead to a vacuum that manifests in various behaviors during adulthood.

Women who grow up without a father or with an emotionally distant father may indeed develop attachment styles that affect their adult relationships. John Bowlby's and Mary Ainsworth's expanded attachment theory suggests that individuals with a history of insecure attachments in childhood may become overly clingy or develop anxious-preoccupied attachment styles in their adult relationships. These individuals often fear abandonment and may require constant reassurance and attention from their partners (Bowlby, 1969; Ainsworth, 1970).

This phenomenon can be understood through the lens of evolutionary psychology, as well—a field I often reference for its insights into human behavior. From an evolutionary standpoint, the attachment system is designed to keep children close to their caregivers for survival. When a child experiences inconsistent caregiving, as might be the case with an absent or inattentive father, they may adapt by becoming overly clingy to secure the needed proximity to their caregiver (Belsky & Fearon, 2002).

In a more practical sense, when considering the role models for a boy on the path to becoming a man, the absence of a father figure can lead to an incomplete picture of how to navigate relationships with women. For a boy to become what might be termed a 'righteous man,'—which we might define as a man who is capable, responsible, and virtuous—he requires a model to emulate. The adage central to the book, "To be one, he has to see one," emphasizes the need for positive male role models to demonstrate the qualities contributing to healthy, stable relationships.

To tie this back to the book's overarching thesis and address the causes of separation and failed relationships, we must look at the developmental history of the individuals involved.

Understanding that clinginess in a woman could indicate a father's absence is to understand the depth of influence early parental engagement, or lack thereof, has on adult relationships. This insight offers a pathway for personal growth and healing and underscores the imperative of present and engaged fatherhood for the psychological development of both boys and girls. Addressing these early relational wounds is critical in cultivating a generation of men capable of forming and maintaining righteous, enduring relationships.

Some women assume we're all the same

The notion that women may generalize men based on their experiences with their fathers is a psychological perspective that merits exploration. According to the psychoanalytic theory proposed by Sigmund Freud, the father-daughter relationship contributes to a woman's relational expectations. The "Electra complex," a term coined by Carl Jung, refers to a girl's psychosexual competition with her mother for possession of her father. While these theories are somewhat outdated and critiqued for their lack of empirical evidence, they have influenced the understanding of familial impacts on future relationships (Jung et al. 1913). The theory of psychoanalysis).

In more contemporary psychology, the father is often seen as a daughter's first male role model. He can significantly influence her perception of men (Nielsen, L. (2012). Father-daughter relationships: Contemporary research and issues). This phenomenon can create a template for what she perceives as "normal" in male behavior, leading to her categorizing men based on this singular model. Suppose her relationship with her father was strained or distant. In that case, she might develop a skewed or mistrustful view of men, expecting disappointment or disengagement as the status quo (East et al., L. (2006).

absence & adolescent development

Conversely, a woman who has experienced an exceptionally positive and perhaps "storybook" relationship with her father might hold men to these lofty standards, which can be as unrealistic as they are unattainable. This idealization can stem from a psychological concept known as the "halo effect," where the overall impression of a person (or, in this case, the father) influences one's feelings and thoughts about that person's character or properties (Nisbett et al., T. D. (1977). The halo effect: Evidence for unconscious alteration of judgments). This halo effect can lead to high or unrealistic expectations in her adult relationships, causing potential conflict when partners inevitably fall short of these idealized benchmarks.

These dynamics are especially relevant in the context of "To Be One He Has to See One; The Only Way a Boy Becomes a Righteous Man." If a woman with such preconceptions enters a relationship and perhaps becomes a mother to a son, these unmet expectations can ripple down to the child. The son's model of being a man is shaped by his direct interactions with his father and his mother's conveyed sentiments and attitudes toward men.

Therefore, the conclusion relevant to the book would emphasize the importance of realistic, balanced, and communicative relationships between fathers and daughters. This sets a precedent for boys and young men to understand and develop healthy relationships with women and vice versa. It highlights that for a boy to grow into a "righteous man," he needs to witness equitable and respectful relationships, learning that men can and do differ widely in character and behavior. Such exposure helps disassemble monolithic stereotypes about men that could be transmitted through maternal disillusionment or idealization. Ultimately, a boy's journey to manhood is significantly influenced by the interplay of relationships within his family and the dismantling of unfounded generalizations. This nurtures his development into a well-rounded, understanding, and respectful individual—qualities at the heart of righteousness.

Some women need constant reassurance

The quest for constant reassurance within a relationship can indeed be symptomatic of deeper psychological issues, often stemming from an upbringing devoid of trust and security. The desire for continuous validation from one's partner may be rooted in an attachment style known as 'anxious attachment,' which, according to Bowlby's Attachment Theory, arises from early experiences with caregivers that were inconsistent with their attention and responsiveness (Bowlby, 1969).

When this need for affirmation manifests in a relationship, it can become a self-fulfilling prophecy; the constant demand for evidence of love may burden the partner, intensifying one's fears of being unlovable or unwanted. In her work on Emotionally Focused Therapy, Dr. Sue Johnson suggests that such neediness patterns can turn affection into an obligation, diminishing its genuine expression and leading to emotional exhaustion (Johnson, 2004).

This behavior affects not just the individual seeking reassurance but also their partner. It can lead to a cycle where the reassured partner, often the man in heterosexual relationships, feels an unrelenting pressure to display affection. If his upbringing lacked a model of a secure, reassuring, and affirming masculine presence—as declared in "To Be One He Has To See One"—he may find this expectation incredibly challenging to meet. The man's discomfort with this dynamic can stem from not having had a role model who demonstrated how to express love and reassurance healthily (Gottman & Silver, 1999).

In the context of "To Be One He Has To See One," the boy's continuous need for reassurance can signal a failure in the relational model provided to him. He may struggle to embody these traits in his relationships if he has not seen a righteous man—a confident figure in his expressions of love and trust. He may neither satisfy his partner's need for security nor affirm his self-worth, perpetuating the cycle of unfulfillment.

To address this within the framework of "To Be One He Has To See One," it is crucial to emphasize the development of trust and secure attachment from an early age. This involves providing boys with positive male role models who demonstrate strong, trustworthy, and emotionally intelligent behavior. By doing so, they can learn to navigate their relationships with a balance of assurance and independence, reducing the likelihood of requiring or eliciting constant reassurance in their future partnerships.

In conclusion, the issue of needing constant reassurance is deeply rooted in early life experiences. Addressing this within the book's narrative underlines the importance of positive role models in breaking the cycle of insecurity and fostering a sense of inherent worth, which can lead to healthier, more stable relationships. To cultivate a generation of righteous men, it is imperative to instill a foundation of trust and self-assurance so they, in turn, can be the steadfast partners and role models needed for the next.

A stagnant relationship

Separation occurs due to an inability of partners to develop closeness; research supports the idea that early parental relationships, especially with fathers, can profoundly influence an individual's approach to adult relationships. According to the Attachment Theory developed by John Bowlby and Mary Ainsworth, the bond formed between a child and their caregiver can set the stage for future relationship patterns. Bowlby's work (1988) suggests that children who experience secure attachment with their caregivers are more likely to develop healthy, autonomous relationships later in life.

In contrast, children with poor parental relationships, particularly with fathers, may struggle with 'avoidant attachment' (Ainsworth, 1973). They may subconsciously maintain emotional distance in adult relationships to protect themselves from the vulnerability and potential rejection that intimacy brings. This avoidance often hinders a relationship's growth. Silverstein and Auerbach (1999), in their work "Deconstructing the Essential Father," argue that the quality of a father's involvement with their children strongly predicts the child's emotional and social well-being.

Further expanding on this, Clea Simon's book "Fatherless Women: How We Change After We Lose Our Dads" (2001) explores the long-lasting impact of the father-daughter relationship. Simon declares that women with absent or unloving fathers often harbor feelings of abandonment and unworthiness, which can erect barriers to intimacy in future relationships.

Therefore, relating this to the book "To Be One, He Has To See One," it is imperative to acknowledge the significance of a father's role in shaping his children's relational blueprints. For a boy to become a "righteous man," as described in the book, he needs to witness and internalize what such a man looks like through his father's model. A righteous man is characterized by his moral convictions and ability to forge deep and meaningful connections with others.

Consequently, repairing and reinforcing the father-child relationship is paramount. The information presented would argue for an active presence and emotional investment from fathers, which is essential for nurturing a boy's capacity to grow into a man who can establish and maintain intimate relationships, hence preventing the cycle of detachment and failed relationships in the future.

Being forced to learn self-reliance

The phenomenon of forced self-reliance and the inability to confide in others has significant implications for the stability of relationships. This behavior often stems from an environment that lacks healthy communication and fails to respect differing opinions, leading to emotional bottlenecks that can contribute to the dissolution of a relationship. The concept of "emotional divorce," as researched by Dr. John Gottman, a leading expert on marital stability, can precede the actual legal divorce and is characterized by a lack of openness and emotional responsiveness between partners (Gottman et al., R. W. (2000). The timing of divorce: Predicting when a couple will divorce over 14 years. Journal of Marriage and Family, 62, 737-745).

Individuals who find themselves in environments where self-expression is stifled may adopt a façade of self-reliance, an adaptation that Gottman's research found can be detrimental to the health of a relationship. Partners who do not feel comfortable sharing their vulnerabilities or concerns can create an emotional distance that is often insurmountable. This behavior is not inherent but learned, and such patterns can be traced back to childhood experiences within the family unit.

Dr. Sue Johnson, creator of Emotionally Focused Therapy (EFT) and a noted author on adult attachment and bonding in couples, asserts that the inability to engage emotionally and the tendency to bottle up feelings are learned behaviors that can be unlearned. Johnson emphasizes the importance of secure attachments and open communication for relationship satisfaction (Johnson et al. (2008). Hold me tight: Seven conversations for a lifetime of love. Little, Brown, Spark).

The consequence of this emotional isolation not only predisposes a relationship to failure but also serves as a poor model for children who observe and internalize these interactions. This is especially true for boys, who are often socialized to prioritize self-reliance over emotional vulnerability. In the context of this book, "To Be One He Has to See One; The Only Way a boy becomes a righteous man," the implications are profound. Boys who witness a lack of healthy communication and emotional support may grow into men who cannot establish and maintain fulfilling relationships.

The book's title submits that exemplars are critical in developing a boy into a man. Thus, a boy must see these qualities modeled to become "righteous"—or healthy, balanced, and just in relationships. If he is instead presented with a paradigm of suppressed communication and enforced self-sufficiency, he may struggle to cultivate the emotional intelligence and openness necessary for a successful partnership.

In conclusion, the cycle of poor communication and the guise of self-reliance as a learned survival mechanism can lead to relationship breakdowns. Addressing these patterns is crucial in nurturing healthy future generations. The message in "To be one, he has to see one" encapsulates the journey from boyhood to manhood and underscores the importance of positive role models in teaching boys how to become men who value and engage in healthy, communicative, and emotionally supportive relationships.

Fear of abandonment

Fear of abandonment is a profound underlying issue that affects relationships, leading to separation and relational failures. This fear often stems from early life experiences or past traumas and can trigger a pattern of avoidance and anxiety within adult relationships. Bowlby's attachment theory, which suggests that early relationships with caregivers can shape expectations and behaviors in later relationships, supports this idea (Bowlby, 1969). Individuals with an anxious or avoidant attachment style may find it challenging to establish deep, enduring bonds, as their fear of being left can sabotage their ability to connect authentically and vulnerably with a partner (Ainsworth & Bowlby, 1991).

Further, according to research by Firestone (2013), fear of abandonment leads to a "defensive self-reliance," where individuals may prematurely exit relationships or avoid intimacy altogether to prevent the possibility of being abandoned. This constant state of relationship flux can prevent the formation of a "great bond," as cultivating deep, meaningful connections takes time and stability.

This behavioral pattern aligns with the principle presented in "To Be One He Has To See One; the only way a boy becomes a righteous man." The journey from boyhood to becoming a 'righteous man' involves learning through example and experience. If a boy observes a pattern of unstable relationships or his caretakers display fear-driven relational behaviors, he may internalize these as usual and replicate them in his adult relationships.

In conclusion, fear of abandonment can create a cycle of short-lived relationships that lack the depth and stability necessary for solid bonds to form. This can perpetuate a legacy of separation and relational dysfunction contrary to the developmental journey outlined in "To Be One He Has To See One." Overcoming this fear and learning to establish secure, reliable connections is integral to breaking the cycle and enabling a boy to grow into a man who embodies and upholds the values of fidelity, strength in commitment, and the ability to nurture enduring relationships. Addressing this issue within the context of the book, we should emphasize the importance of modeling healthy relationships to the younger generation and providing them with the tools and understanding necessary to overcome their fears of abandonment. This prepares them not just for relationships but for forming a righteous character.

Some women have commitment issues

The role of early parental relationships in shaping an individual's capacity for commitment in adulthood has been widely studied in psychological literature. According to attachment theory, as postulated by John Bowlby and later expanded by Mary Ainsworth, the bond a child forms with their caregiver—typically a parent—sets the stage for future relationship patterns (Bowlby, 1969; Ainsworth, 1979). This foundational relationship often serves as a blueprint for relationships, how trust is built, and how affection is expressed and received.

Numerous studies suggest that the quality of a woman's relationship with her father can significantly influence her future romantic relationships. For instance, a study by Nielsen

(2012) supports the assertion that daughters who report good communication and a high level of trust with their fathers are likelier to form secure and trusting relationships with their partners. Conversely, suppose the father-daughter relationship is fraught with neglect, inconsistency, or abuse. In that case, it can lead to what is known as an insecure attachment style, which can manifest as commitment issues in later life (Harris & Vernon, 2017).

The dynamic between the father and the mother is equally influential. Daughters closely observe and internalize the interactions between their parents. If a father displays respect, affection, and commitment in his relationship with the mother, it often sets a positive example. However, witnessing a tumultuous or distant relationship between parents may sow seeds of doubt and mistrust about romantic partnerships (Fisher et al., 2003).

"To Be One He Has To See One; the Only Way a Boy Becomes a Righteous Man" underscores the importance of modeling solid and committed relationships for children. The adage "to be one, he has to see one" reflects that for a boy to become a righteous and committed man, he must witness such characteristics exemplified, particularly in his father or male role models. If he sees his father honoring commitments and treating women with respect, it is more likely that he will adopt these behaviors in his relationships.

In conclusion, the early relational environment that a girl experiences with her father can play a pivotal role in her future romantic life. If we wish to cultivate a generation of men capable of commitment and righteousness in their relationships, it is incumbent upon fathers and male role models to demonstrate these qualities. This idea reinforces the book's core message that the integrity and commitment observed by children in their formative years are critical in shaping the adults they will become, thereby perpetuating a legacy of healthy, stable relationships.

Some women are too hypersexual

In the discourse on family breakdowns, one nuanced aspect often overlooked is the role of sexual dynamics in the degradation of relational stability. This is not solely about overt infidelity but involves a deeper psychological pattern where hypersexuality and the eagerness to please a partner can overshadow the foundations of mutual respect and genuine affection.

The confusion between sex and love, and the consequent conflation of being liked with being respected, can be a significant factor in the erosion of a relationship. According to M. Gary Neuman, in his book "The Truth about Cheating," emotional dissatisfaction is a leading cause of infidelity, with sexual dissatisfaction much further down the list (Neuman, 2008). This suggests that the issues often have deeper emotional roots than physical expressions.

Furthermore, studies have shown that individuals who use sex as a means to feel reassured may inadvertently undermine the potential for a genuine connection, mistaking transient attention for lasting affection. This behavior can stem from a variety of psychological issues, such as low self-esteem or attachment disorders, which are discussed in depth by Dr. Sue Johnson in her work "Hold Me Tight: Seven Conversations for a Lifetime of Love" (Johnson, 2008). Johnson explains that such behavior often reflects a deep-seated fear of abandonment or a longing for validation.

Women's hypersexual behavior often surfaces in public discourse as a topic mired in controversy and moral judgment. However, beneath the superficial layers of these conversations are complex psychological patterns and societal factors contributing to such behavior. Hypersexuality in women can be understood not merely as an issue of morality or choice but as a multifaceted phenomenon often deeply rooted in early familial dynamics, particularly the absence of a father figure.

Causes and Connections: The Absent Father Link: The absence of a father—or a nurturing, stable paternal influence—during a girl's formative years can have profound repercussions on her development. A myriad of studies suggest that fatherless women may engage in hypersexual behavior as a subconscious attempt to fill the void of paternal affection and attention. This search for validation and love can become misconstrued, leading to the belief that sexual attention equates to a much-needed and missed emotional connection.

Dangers of Hypersexuality: Hypersexuality carries with it inherent dangers that extend beyond the physical risks of sexually transmitted infections or unplanned pregnancies. Emotionally, it can lead to a cycle of self-objectification, where a woman's self-worth becomes entangled with her sexual desirability to others, potentially leading to emotional distress and mental health issues such as depression or anxiety.

The Impact on Children: A Single Mother's Influence: When a single mother displays hypersexual behavior, the impact on her children can be significant and lasting. A daughter may come to model this behavior, perceiving it as a standard means of interacting with the world and seeking affection. She may also develop skewed perceptions of intimacy and self-worth, associating love with sexual behavior. For a son raised without a father, witnessing his mother's hypersexuality can be equally formative. It can influence his understanding of respect, consent, and the value of women, potentially shaping how he perceives and engages with women in his life.

Navigating the Influence: Steps Towards Healing: Acknowledging the link between the father's absence and hypersexuality is a crucial step in addressing the roots of this behavior. Therapeutic interventions that focus on building self-esteem and developing healthy relationship patterns can be instrumental for women grappling with these issues. Encouraging positive male role models for children, alongside fostering open discussions about self-worth and healthy sexuality, can also mitigate the cycle of hypersexuality.

In understanding women's hypersexual behavior, we must adopt a compassionate lens, recognizing the profound influence of early familial experiences and the power of societal structures. Within this understanding, we can unravel the threads of behavior, address the underlying causes, and ultimately guide individuals and families toward healthier, more fulfilling ways of relating to one another and themselves.

The consequences of such dynamics are especially pertinent when considering the upbringing of boys and their development into men. "To be one, he has to see one; the only way a boy becomes a righteous man" implies that the modeling of relationships that boys observe profoundly impacts their future behavior and understanding of love, respect, and intimacy.

Suppose a boy grows up witnessing relationships where sexual behavior is used as a barometer for love and respect or where affection is commoditized. In that case, he may adopt a skewed perspective of what constitutes a healthy relationship. In contrast, witnessing relationships built on mutual respect, emotional support, and clear boundaries provides a blueprint for positive interactions in his future relationships.

Hypersexuality can manifest in various behaviors and patterns that might be witnessed by children, sometimes even without the full awareness of the mothers or the women exhibiting them.

Hypersexual behaviors children observe

Multiple Romantic Partners: Children are incredibly attentive. When you think they are not or think they don't notice, they pop up and remind you to be more aware and careful of your words and actions. Children can notice various romantic partners entering and exiting their lives. Although they may not be explained or introduced as an intimate partner, it is still a potential bond with another influential person that makes an impact, no matter how trivial or minuscule it may be. This can be confusing and destabilizing, as they may form attachments or feel abandoned repeatedly.

Sexualized Appearance and Behavior: When children see a primary female caregiver consistently presenting themselves in a highly sexualized manner, it may distort their perception of normative adult behavior and dress.

Inappropriate Boundaries: Children may be exposed to adult sexual behavior, discussions, or displays of affection that are not age-appropriate, leading to an early and confusing introduction to sexuality.

Neglect of Parental Duties: In some cases, a mother's hypersexual behavior can lead to the decay of children's emotional or physical needs, as the pursuit of sexual relationships may take precedence over time spent with children.

Online Presence: A mother's hypersexual behavior may also manifest in how she presents herself online, through social media, or dating sites, which children could inadvertently observe.

Reckless Behavior: Engaging in risky sexual behaviors without concern for safety or the presence of children, such as leaving children unattended to meet a partner or bringing new partners into the home environment without proper consideration.

Substance Abuse: Sometimes, hypersexuality is linked with substance abuse, where children might witness a correlation between a mother's intoxication and lowered inhibitions leading to sexual activity.

Interpersonal Conflict: Children may be exposed to the conflict that arises from a mother's romantic or sexual relationships, such as arguments, jealousy, or even violence, which can have a traumatic effect.

Emotional Volatility: The highs and lows associated with unstable relationships can create an emotionally charged and unpredictable home environment.

Sexualizing Relationships: Observing a mother who consistently interprets male attention or kindness as sexual can teach children to misconstrue platonic relationships as inherently sexual.

Sexting or Explicit Communication: Children might accidentally witness explicit text messages or hear phone conversations of a sexual nature.

Addressing hypersexuality, particularly in single-parent homes, requires a careful and nuanced approach that respects the complexities of individual situations. Mothers need to be aware of the impact of their behaviors on their children and seek support, if necessary, to maintain a healthy and appropriate environment for their families. Open communication, education, and setting boundaries can help mitigate the effects on children and guide them toward understanding healthy expressions of sexuality.

The conclusion to be drawn is that the perpetuation of healthy relationship dynamics is not just a private matter but a societal imperative. As such, it is crucial to address these underlying issues for the sake of individual family units and the collective good. Education on healthy relationships, communication, and emotional intelligence must become integral in the narrative of personal development, particularly for young men.

Addressing these psychological patterns that contribute to relationship dissolution, "To Be One He Has To See One" can serve as a clarion call for the importance of providing positive examples of manhood, including the capacity for emotional intimacy, respect, and a healthy expression of sexuality. Only then can we hope to reduce the incidence of separation rooted in the misalignment of sex and love, thereby fostering a generation of men who understand the profound difference between being liked and being respected.

Some women have deep resentment towards men

One significant issue in addressing the deeper causes of separation and failed relationships is the development of resentment toward men. This resentment can stem from various experiences or observations—or the lack thereof. A negative encounter with a male figure can leave an indelible mark on one's perception, leading to generalization and low expectations toward men.

Psychological literature often references the concept of 'schema'—cognitive frameworks that help individuals organize and interpret information. According to Young, Klosko, and Weishaar's seminal work, "Schema Therapy: A Practitioner's Guide" (2003), negative schemas can develop from early adverse experiences and heavily influence one's expectations and interactions in adult relationships. If a person has experienced or witnessed mistreatment by men, whether through a direct relationship or observation of a parental figure, it can contribute to the formation of a negative schema (Young et al., 2003).

Moreover, the absence of positive male role models can further compound these perceptions. In families where the father figure is absent—due to separation, divorce, or other circumstances—children may grow up with a void in their understanding of male behavior. The lack of a father or a positive male figure can create a gap, which may be filled with societal stereotypes rather than real-life positive interactions. In "Fatherless America: Confronting Our Most Urgent Social Problem" (1995), David Blankenhorn discusses the societal impact of fatherless homes, underscoring the potential for developing a skewed perspective of men when paternal figures are absent.

This generalized resentment and expectation can create a self-fulfilling prophecy within relationships. Monroe, Rohde, Seeley, and Lewinsohn's study in the Journal of Abnormal Psychology (1999) suggests that negative relationship expectations can lead to a heightened perception of relationship difficulties, perpetuating conflict and dissatisfaction.

Bringing this back to the context of "To Be One, He Has to See One," the implications are profound. The book's title suggests modeling behavior is essential in developing an individual's character and expectations. The phrase "the only way a boy becomes a righteous man" implies the necessity of witnessing virtuous behavior, particularly from male role models such as a father. These examples of chivalry, kindness, and strength of character are necessary for young men to embody these traits.

In conclusion, it is crucial to address the role of male figures in young people's lives to foster healthier relationships and reduce the separation rate due to these deep-seated resentments and expectations. Providing positive male role models, whether within the family or through community mentoring programs, could mitigate the development of negative schemas. This aligns with the central thesis of the book —that in order for a boy to mature into a 'righteous man,' he must have access to and recognize such examples in his life. Through this, we can uplift expectations and dissolve generalized resentments, laying the groundwork for more successful and fulfilling relationships.

A woman's attraction to older men

To further elaborate on the notion of women gravitating toward partners who are the same age or near the age of their fathers, we can draw upon psychological theories and research. This phenomenon can be partly attributed to the 'imprinting' or 'template' theories, which suggest that early parental figures establish a prototype for future romantic attraction. Freud's concept of the 'Oedipus complex' touches on this, proposing that children feel a subconscious attraction to the opposite-sex parent. However, in the context of adult relationships, this manifests more as a search for familiarity and comfort rather than a direct psychosexual attraction (Freud, S. (1910). The Interpretation of Dreams. MacMillan).

There is nothing intrinsically problematic about age-disparate relationships. Still, issues arise when women pursue such relationships as a subconscious means to fill a void left by an absent or deficient father figure. This is explored in the attachment theory, which posits that early interactions with caregivers form the basis for future relationship dynamics (Bowlby, J. (1969). Attachment. Attachment and Loss: Vol. 1. Loss. Basic Books).

The quest for an older partner to compensate for paternal shortcomings can lead to a dynamic where unmet, often unconscious, expectations burden the relationship. Women may seek not just a partner but a protector, mentor, or authority figure—roles that should be distinct from those of a romantic partner. This can create an imbalance in the relationship, fostering dependency and possibly leading to its deterioration if a younger or same-age partner cannot, or chooses not, to fulfill these expectations.

This is relevant to the book "To Be One He Has to See One." If we accept the premise that a boy's journey to righteous manhood is influenced by his role models—mainly male figures—then the absence or inadequacy of a father can have significant implications. It affects not only the boy's development but also the future expectations and relationship dynamics of women within his sphere.

Concluding this point in the context of the book's theme, it is essential to recognize that the pursuit of older men as surrogates for paternal figures by women is symptomatic of a deeper societal issue—the absence of strong, positive male role models. This gap in mentorship and guidance can result in a cycle where women seek to fill the void through relationships with older who may not be willing or unavailable, and sons grow up without a clear blueprint for becoming 'righteous men.' Addressing this issue requires fostering environments where boys have access to and can model after responsible, mature, and emotionally present men—ensuring that when they grow, they can embody the virtues that would make them exemplary partners, fathers, and leaders in their own right.

Though separation may emerge as a logical resolution, we cannot ignore its adverse impact on children. As the adage goes, the ideal is that "the family is the security of society," and forging a family through a relationship is seen as the standard model. However, we recognize that maintaining such relationships is not always feasible and that, at times, separation may serve the best interests of all involved.

This chapter, "Unseen Currents," lets us reflect on its essence and urgent call to action. Our journey through these pages was not to assign blame or cast aspersions on those navigating the treacherous waters of personal relationships. Instead, it illuminated the profound impacts a father's presence

—or the lack thereof—can have on the emotional and developmental currents shaping our lives.

Indeed, absent fathers' unseen, often unacknowledged influence reverberates through the lives of both men and women, manifesting in their choices and patterns. This is not an indictment but a stark observation supported by logic and statistics. Our purpose is not to criticize but to explore every avenue to acknowledge every factor contributing to this societal challenge.

To truly understand the consequences of paternal absence, we must recognize the child at the center of this storm—vulnerable and too often neglected in the chaos of adult struggles. The fallout is unmistakable: a regression in childhood development, surging insecurities, and diminishing potential as both boys and girls grapple with the absence of a guiding figure.

This book stands as a clarion call to address the crisis of absentee fathers and shake the complacency of those who have neglected their responsibilities. We must confront the uncomfortable statistics and the harsh realities and then, most crucially, act. Our vision is clear: to cultivate righteous relationships built on the bedrock of strong values, to strive for unity, and to nurture a familial environment where sacrifice, communication, and teamwork reign supreme.

In echoing the wisdom of Dr. Myles Monroe, "Society is the reflection of the conditions of the family," we must confront the troubling image that our society reflects us—an image marred by failure, excuses, and a lack of resolve. It reflects men struggling to mature without role models and families splintered by shortcuts and false hopes.

Nevertheless, amidst this stark reality lies an undeniable truth: To become, one must witness. Through example, we can forge a path to rediscovery, recovery, and rebuilding. As the nucleus of society, the family holds the key to a stable and thriving nation. Our final message is one of hope and determination: To be one, one must see one. Moreover, this witnessing shows that the family, the cornerstone of our society, can be restored and strengthened.

We invite you to turn the page, continue this crucial conversation, and join us to heal and fortify the most fundamental unit of our community—the Men in our family.

References to Consider:

- Ainsworth, M. D. S., & Bowlby, J. (1991). An ethological approach to personality development. *American Psychologist, 46*(4), 333–341.

- Bowlby, J. (1969). Attachment and Loss: Vol. 1. Attachment. New York: Basic Books.

- Firestone, L. (2013). Fear of Intimacy and Closeness in Relationships. PsychAlive. Retrieved from https://www.psychalive.org/fear-of-intimacy-and-closeness-in-relationships/

WHO DEFINED THE ROLE OF THE FATHER

Here is a question I am asking out of curiosity and random thoughts: Who decides our role as a father- us as men, women, children, society, or our cultures?

The role of fathers, or fatherhood, is influenced and shaped by a combination of factors, including personal choice, societal norms, cultural expectations, and the dynamics within individual families.

HERE IS A CLOSER LOOK AT THE INFLUENCES:

Personal Choice (Men themselves): Ultimately, an individual man decides how he will perform his role as a father. This includes his level of involvement, the values he wants to impart, and how he balances fatherhood with other aspects of his life. Personal beliefs, ethics, and priorities are significant in these decisions.

Societal Norms: Society at large has expectations and norms regarding what a father's role should be. These norms have evolved and continue to do so. In many modern societies, there is a growing emphasis on fathers being more emotionally available and involved in their children's lives compared to past generations, where the father's role was often primarily seen as a provider and disciplinarian.

Cultural Expectations: Different cultures have varying expectations for fathers. In some cultures, the father's traditional role as the primary breadwinner and disciplinarian is still prevalent. In contrast, in others, there is a strong emphasis on fathers being actively involved in all aspects of child-rearing. Cultural beliefs and traditions can significantly influence how a man perceives and performs his role as a father.

Family Dynamics: Family dynamics, including the relationship with the child's other parent and the needs of the children, can significantly influence a father's role. For example, in a single-parent family, a father might have to take on a broader range of responsibilities. In other cases, the division of responsibilities and roles between parents can be influenced by factors such as each parent's work schedule, skills and interests, and approach to parenting.

Children's Expectations and Needs: Children can shape their father's role through their expectations and needs. A father might adapt his role based on each child's unique personality, interests, and needs.

Influence of Extended Family and Community: The extended family and community can also have an impact, offering models, expectations, and sometimes pressure regarding how a father should act.

Economic and Social Conditions: Broader economic and social conditions, such as the availability of paternity leave, workplace policies, and societal attitudes towards gender roles, also play a significant role in defining fatherhood.

In conclusion, the role of a father is not determined by a single factor. Instead, it is a dynamic interplay of personal choices, societal and cultural influences, family dynamics, and children's evolving needs and expectations. Fathers today often navigate a complex landscape as they seek to define and fulfill their role in a way that aligns with their values, their children's needs, and the expectations of their society and culture.

Various resources can be consulted to support and further explore the various influences on fathers' roles. These include academic research, books, articles, and organizations focused on parenting and fatherhood.

Below are some resources that can provide more insight and information:

Academic Journals and Research Papers:

- *Journal of Family Psychology*: Offers research on family dynamics and roles.

- *Fathering: A Journal of Theory, Research, and Practice about Men as Fathers*: This journal focuses explicitly on fatherhood and can provide insights into how the role of fathers is viewed and studied academically.

Books:

- "The New Father: A Dad's Guide to the First Year" by Armin A. Brott offers practical advice and explores the emotional, financial, and physical changes a new father might experience.

- "Fatherhood: Evolution and Human Paternal Behavior," by Peter B. Gray and Kermyt G. Anderson, delves into the evolutionary aspects of fatherhood and provides a broader understanding of how father roles have developed and changed over time.

Organizations:

- National Fatherhood Initiative (NFI): This organization provides resources and researches the importance of a father's role in the family.

- Fathers.com: Sponsored by the National Center for Fathering, this website offers articles, tips, and resources for fathers.

Online Articles and Blogs:

- Websites like Psychology Today, The Good Men Project, and HuffPost Parents often feature articles about fatherhood that discuss contemporary issues and perspectives.

Government and Educational Resources:

- Many government websites offer resources and information about parenting and fatherhood. For example, the U.S. Department of Health & Human Services has resources for fathers.

- Universities often publish studies and articles about family dynamics and parenting through their psychology, sociology, or family studies departments.

Social Media and Online Forums:

- Platforms like Reddit, Facebook groups, and other online communities for fathers can provide insight into dads' real-life experiences and perspectives in the present day.

Documentaries and Podcasts:

- Numerous documentaries and podcasts explore fatherhood from various cultural, social, and personal perspectives, offering in-depth looks at the challenges and joys of fatherhood.

Cultural and Sociological Texts:

- Books and papers that delve into the cultural and sociological aspects of parenting and gender roles can offer a deeper understanding of how societal norms and cultural practices influence fatherhood.

Books

"Fatherhood: Evolution and Human Paternal Behavior" by Peter B. Gray and Kermyt G. Anderson - This book provides an evolutionary perspective on fatherhood, examining how human paternal behavior compares with that of other species and how it varies across human societies.

"The Role of the Father in Child Development" edited by Michael E. Lamb - A seminal work that compiles research on the father's role across various developmental stages of a child's life, offering insights into how fathers contribute to the emotional, social, and cognitive development of their children.

"Do Fathers Matter? What Science Is Telling Us About the Parent We've Overlooked" by Paul Raeburn - Raeburn synthesizes a wide range of scientific research to argue for the significant impact fathers have on their children, from conception through adulthood.

"Fathering: Masculinity and the Embodiment of Care" by Gillian Ranson explores how men negotiate their identities as fathers and caregivers within the context of societal expectations about masculinity and fatherhood.

"The Daddy Shift: How Stay-at-Home Dads, Breadwinning Moms, and Shared Parenting Are Transforming the American Family" by Jeremy A. Smith discusses the changing dynamics of American families, focusing on the rise of stay-at-home dads and how these shifts challenge traditional notions of fatherhood and masculinity.

Academic Papers

"The Effects of Father Involvement: An Updated Research Summary of the Evidence" by Sarah Allen and Kerry Daly - This paper summarizes recent research findings on the impact of father involvement on children and families, highlighting the positive benefits of active fathering.

"Involved Fatherhood and Men's Adult Development: Provisional Balances" by Michael E. Lamb examines the impact of fatherhood on men's development, arguing that active involvement in parenting leads to positive outcomes for fathers.

"Masculinities and Fatherhood: The Case of Fair and Equal Parenting" by Andrea Doucet - Doucet explores how fathers who engage in "fair and equal parenting" navigate and negotiate their masculinities within the context of their family lives.

"Paternal Participation in Child Care and Its Effects on Children's Self-Esteem and Attitudes toward Gendered Roles" by Elizabeth Thomson, Sara McLanahan, and Robert L. Hanson - This study investigates how fathers' involvement in child care influences children's self-esteem and their perceptions of gender roles.

"Gender and Parenthood: Biological and Social Scientific Perspectives" edited by W. Bradford Wilcox and Kathleen Kovner Kline - This collection of essays examines how biology and social science intersect to shape parenting practices and gender roles within families.

These works contribute to a deeper understanding of the multifaceted nature of fatherhood and parenting within various societal and cultural contexts. They offer valuable insights for scholars, students, and anyone interested in the dynamics of family life and gender roles. They combine scholarly research, practical advice, personal experiences, and theoretical exploration to comprehensively view the factors influencing fathers' roles in different contexts.

FATHER & MOTHER BALANCE

"When men abandon the upbringing of their children to their wives, they suffer a significant loss.
What they lose is a possibility of growth in themselves for being human, which the stimulation of
bringing up children uses."

- Ashley Montague Anthropologist, 1964

When a man delegates the sacred duty of raising his children solely to the woman, he inflicts grave injustice upon himself. He forsakes a divine opportunity for personal development—a chance to cultivate the very essence of his humanity. You see, in the nurturing and upbringing of one's offspring, a man finds an unmatched stimulus that can shape and refine his character. Through the trials, the joys, the tribulations, and the triumphs of fatherhood, a man indeed confronts the full spectrum of his capacities for compassion, understanding, and growth.

Moreover, in this neglect, he unwittingly weakens the family unit—the cornerstone of our community. Maternal and paternal influence balance is vital to a child's healthy development. When a father is absent and relinquishes his role and responsibility, he not only deprives himself of a profound journey of self-discovery but also robs his children of the critical life lessons that only a father can impart. To be fully human to rise to the heights of our potential, we must embrace the total weight of our responsibilities, not as a burden but as a privilege—a path to true enlightenment and strength.

The essence of fatherhood extends far beyond provision and protection; it fundamentally encompasses the respect and love a father displays towards the mother of his children. The ancient Stoic philosopher Epictetus once stated, "What concerns me is not the way things are, but rather the way people think things are." This reflects the profound impact of a father's behavior on a child's perception of relationships and respect.

For many fathers, the most challenging aspect of parenting may not be the myriad tasks of child-rearing but their interactions with the child's mother. This difficulty is compounded for those who have yet to witness a healthy male-female relationship or are uncertain how to engage with the mother respectfully and positively.

From a psychological standpoint, the period before a child is conceived is crucial. Research suggests that many men, particularly those from environments with a "quantity over quality" mentality regarding sexual encounters, fail to consider the long-term implications of their partner choice. Dr. Terri Conley from the University of Michigan argues that partner selection is a critical determinant of relationship satisfaction and stability, influencing family dynamics and child outcomes.

The historically promiscuous approach—exemplified by the maxim "Turn nothing down but your collar"—encourages young men to engage in careless relationships, often overlooking the more profound qualities in a partner. The Stoic philosopher Seneca would likely admonish such imprudence: "We are more often frightened than hurt, and we suffer more from imagination than from reality." The reality of reckless behavior can lead to diseases or unintended parenthood, both of which have lifelong consequences.

In my journey, a mentor challenged me to consider whether my partner was genuinely suited for parenthood and life partnership before procreation. I had to confront the fact that I had overlooked essential questions about her education, family relationships, ambitions, and character—factors crucial to a harmonious and supportive relationship.

The foundation of a relationship should not be likened to quicksand but to solid ground. Whether or not to raise children together should be approached with the same diligence as a business partnership. A father's mindset often shifts upon having children as he considers his legacy and the values he imparts.

The "family as business" concept stresses the importance of a partner's inner qualities over mere physical attraction. Sociologist Dr. Pepper Schwartz of the University of Washington highlights the value of mutual respect, shared goals, and compatible parenting styles in forming a stable family unit.

Furthermore, how a father communicates with the mother of his children sets a precedent. Children are keen observers and can sense the energy between their parents, even in their absence. Their perceptions of love and security are greatly influenced by the affection and respect they observe, as noted by child development experts. For instance, witnessing acts of love, such as holding hands or sharing a kiss, can impart a profound sense of security.

The Stoic idea of maintaining one's composure becomes paramount when disagreements arise- as they inevitably will. Marcus Aurelius, a Stoic emperor, advised, "How much more grievous are the consequences of anger than the causes of it." Thus, a father must always remain composed in the face of conflict, for the children are watching, learning how to handle adversity and disagreement.

Lastly, intimacy is not merely physical but a binding responsibility contract for at least 18 years. The gravity of this commitment necessitates deep, meaningful communication and shared values between partners. This is not only for the good of the potential child but for the mutual growth and happiness of both partners involved.

In conclusion, the father's treatment of the mother is a powerful lesson to his children. It's an instruction in love, respect, and choosing a partner wisely—tasks passed down in words and demonstrated in daily actions and decisions. Seneca once said, "Our actions are like ships which we may watch set out to sea and not know when or with what cargo they will return to port." Fathers must be mindful of the cargo they carry, and the course they set, for their children's eyes are upon them, charting their paths by his example.

DO'S AND DON'TS

PARENTING INSIGHTS:

Guiding Principles and Behavioral Outcomes

The Nurturing Fathers program's discourse on "Do's, Don'ts, and Consequences" significantly resonates with me. This particular chapter illuminated a crucial aspect of parenting—how to ensure our children's appropriate behavior in our absence. This challenge is universal among parents: How do we influence our children to maintain consistent behavior whether we're present or not?

A poignant example occurred when I received an email from my son's teacher detailing behavior that seemed uncharacteristic of the child I knew. This instance wasn't the first and certainly wouldn't be the last, evoking memories of my childhood when my teachers would present a "behavior folder" at parent-teacher conferences, much to my parents' dismay.

My approach with my son was to foster open communication rather than resorting to the punitive reactions I experienced as a child. After calmly reading the email to him and expressing that he wasn't in trouble, we discussed his school behavior and expectations. As Dale Carnegie emphasizes in "How to Win Friends and Influence People," it's pivotal to remember that children are often a product of their environment and act based on what they don't know. We must be present and guide them constructively.

Statistical support for such approaches is clear. According to a study published in the "Journal of Family Psychology," positive reinforcement and consistent communication are far more effective in shaping a child's behavior long-term than punitive measures (Snyder, 2005). The American Psychological Association also underlines the importance of clear communication and consistent expectations to help children develop self-regulation skills (APA, 2012).

Moreover, research from the National Institute of Child Health and Human Development shows that children who receive high-quality parenting—marked by a warm, nurturing environment combined with clear guidelines—are more likely to develop positive social behaviors and lower levels of problematic behaviors (NICHD Early Child Care Research Network, 2008).

In implementing these strategies, I understood that it wasn't just about being a disciplinarian; it was about being a role model and mentor. The "Nurturing Fathers" program, along with the profound wisdom of Carnegie, imparts that effective parenting requires not just setting boundaries but also engaging actively with our children to teach them how to navigate those boundaries with respect and understanding.

In conclusion, children learn and imitate behaviors they observe, and it's imperative that, as parents, we consistently demonstrate the values we wish to instill. By actively participating in their lives with guidance and understanding, we stand a better chance of nurturing well-rounded individuals who act responsibly, whether under our watchful eye or not.

A clear understanding of this principle can significantly simplify parenting and holding children accountable. I approached my son with a question that I believe many parents overlook: "What, to you, defines 'cool'?" His response arrived after a thoughtful pause: attractiveness, trendy attire, the use of slang, and humor.

This exchange was revealing, not for what was said, but for what was left unsaid. When I probed for uncool behaviors, he drew a blank. This was a pivotal moment for me, realizing that our children might not naturally make connections between actions and their social perceptions.

Seeking to guide him, I asked if dishonesty was 'cool.' His immediate response was negative. We continued this dialogue, addressing punctuality, academic diligence, and total effort. He quickly understood these qualities were not just obligations but integral to one's character and reputation—being 'cool.'

To reinforce this, we discussed the potential consequences of his choices. I explained how dedication to his studies would elevate his social standing among peers and ensure academic advancement and intellectual growth. Conversely, we explored the likely outcomes of neglecting his education, illustrating how such choices could adversely affect his future.

Professionals in child development underscore the importance of such conversations. Dr. Michele Borba, an educational psychologist and author, asserts that children thrive on clear expectations and understanding their rationale (Borba, "Un-Selfie: Why Empathetic Kids Succeed in Our All-About-Me World," 2016). By engaging in discussions that connect behavior with outcomes, we provide a blueprint for children that aligns with their values and aspirations.

I urge fellow fathers to adopt this approach. By clarifying what we expect from our children and delineating the image they aspire to embody, we create a framework for accountability. It's essential to acknowledge that adapting to this method may initially be challenging; it's a departure from the norm. However, the long-term benefits for the parent-child relationship can be profound.

Patience is vital in this process. We are aiming for success over time, not instant results. By steadily modeling and reinforcing these concepts, we can foster a sense of responsibility and 'coolness' in character that our children will carry into their futures.

The capacity to regulate our emotional responses is a challenge that many grapple with. While our feelings are often spontaneous and difficult to control, our reactions to those emotions are within our power to manage. The premise that individuals react as they do due to a lack of guidance in emotional response has some merit. Educational psychologist John Gottman emphasizes the importance of inspirational coaching, which can influence how one learns to respond to feelings (Gottman, 1997). As a father, embodying composure, patience, and a problem-solving mindset is paramount. Fathers often strive to be exemplars of emotional regulation for their children.

In stressful situations, detaching oneself to gain a clearer perspective is valuable. Taking a step back to view the problem from a "3000-foot view" allows for a more objective assessment. A study in the "Journal of Personality and Social Psychology" suggests that psychological distancing can help individuals regulate their emotional responses and reduce aggression (Mischkowski et al., 2012).

Awareness of the specific triggers, whether certain words or tones, is crucial in managing responses. The recommendation to take three deep breaths aligns with mindfulness techniques, which have been shown to reduce emotional reactivity (Zeidan et al., 2010). These practices enable an individual to return to the present moment and address the situation more calmly.

Discipline, although not immediately gratifying, is essential for growth and order. The anecdote of the penny underscores the importance of attention to detail and the concept that leadership often requires attending to even the smallest of tasks. This aligns with research that suggests noticing and listening to the environment is a component of conscientiousness, a personality trait associated with leadership (Judge et al., 2002).

The nightly routine of ensuring everything is in its place within the home embodies the adage, "You have to be able to lay a hand on it." This principle highlights the value of orderliness and preparedness, reflecting a proactive rather than reactive approach to parenthood and leadership.

When it comes to discipline and correction, the distinction is critical. Punishment alone can only be effective with the educational aspect of correction. Research in developmental psychology supports the notion that constructive discipline that teaches responsibility is more effective than punitive measures (Kazdin, 2005).

As a father, taking on the roles of coach, trainer, motivational speaker, and leader requires a balance between friendliness and authority. Children must understand that discipline stems from a place of care and guidance. According to Baumrind's research on parenting styles, authoritative parenting—which combines warmth with firmness—is associated with positive outcomes in children (Baumrind, 1966).

In conclusion, discipline is about instilling moral and mental fortitude and ensuring each family member has a role and place. The parent is responsible for establishing order when things go awry, shaping an environment conducive to growth and character development. Through their example and teachings, fathers have the unique opportunity to foster resilience and responsibility in their children, setting the groundwork for their future successes.

HOW DOES A MAN BECOME A FATHER

The transition from man to father is a profound journey that stretches beyond the mere biological act of procreation. Exploring this transformation involves understanding the difference between siring offspring and embracing the full spectrum of fatherhood.

Biologically, a man becomes a father when he contributes his DNA to create a new life (Marsiglio, W., Amato, P., Day, R.D., & Lamb, M.E., 2000). Yet, an authentic father's role is not fulfilled merely at conception; it is a lifelong commitment that requires constant learning, growth, and adaptation.

Societal misconceptions about fatherhood often focus on the superficial rewards of parenting, overshadowing the integral roles, responsibilities, and accountability inherent in fathering a child. Today's media can bombard men with images that objectify women and emphasize sexual conquest, which can lead to irresponsible behaviors and unintended parenthood without a complete understanding of the consequences (Kiselica, M.S., & Morrill-Richards, M., 2007).

I vividly recall the life-altering moment when I learned I would be a father at 26. The initial exhilaration was quickly tempered by a rush of practical concerns—where we would live, what car to drive, and how to provide the right environment for my child. Society's expectations weighed heavily upon me at that time, but there was little guidance on how to meet them.

I faced the daunting realization that it is challenging to deliver on expectations when you need a model to follow. Like many men, I had to navigate fatherhood without a blueprint. This is a common scenario, given that many children grow up without a father figure, lacking the direct instruction and example needed to guide their journey into fatherhood (National Fatherhood Initiative, 2021).

As my child's birth approached, my relationship with my partner evolved, and new expectations arose. I had never been taught these tasks, yet there was an assumption that I should instinctively know how to perform them.

The pressure to know everything and meet every demand can strain a relationship, sometimes leading to conflict. This tension can be likened to someone using a vending machine. They invest their emotional, physical, and financial currencies anticipating a desired snack and treat, known as a specific outcome. When the machine malfunctions, that triggers a reaction. The machine's malfunction is interpreted as unmet expectations, and frustration ensues, and the 'vending machine,' being the people in your life, may be subjected to anger and aggression. It's a painful reality that some men know how to father a child but are at a loss when it comes to raising one, often due to the absence of their fathers as role models (Palkovitz, R., 2002). Nonetheless, a biological father's lack of guidance doesn't seal one's fate.

For men forging their path in fatherhood without a personal example to follow, it is crucial to seek out resources and role models. This can be through mentorship, educational books on fatherhood, support groups, or texts offering philosophical or ethical parenting guidance (Lamb, M.E., 2010). Every man must ask himself how he wants to be remembered by his child and strive to embody that ideal.

Becoming a father is a transformative experience that encompasses more than genetics. It is about nurturing, guiding, and committing to the well-being of another human life. A father's legacy is not just in the DNA he passes on but in the daily acts of love, strength, and wisdom he imparts to his children.

MOTIVATION BEHIND EMBRACING FATHERHOOD

A MESSAGE TO THE NEXT GENERATION OF YOUNG LADIES & YOUNG MEN

The decision to embrace fatherhood is a complex and deeply personal journey unique to each individual. The motivations behind this choice vary widely, reflecting a blend of cultural, religious, biological, and emotional factors. We will explore the diverse reasons that lead men to take on the role of a father, starting with the intricate subjects of beliefs, instincts, and desires that shape this decision.

Cultural and religious beliefs are at the heart of many decisions to become a father. In numerous cultures worldwide, fatherhood is revered as a sacred duty, a milestone marking the transition from youth to adulthood, or a responsibility endowed with spiritual significance. For men influenced by these cultural and religious contexts, becoming a father is more than a personal choice; it fulfills a societal expectation or a spiritual calling. This perspective often instills in men a sense of duty and purpose that transcends personal aspirations, anchoring the role of fatherhood in a larger communal and spiritual continuity framework.

Conversely, some men are drawn to fatherhood by the fundamental biological instinct to procreate and pass on their genetic legacy. This primal urge, deeply embedded in human nature, drives the continuation of the species and the preservation of genetic material. For these individuals, fatherhood is a natural step in the life cycle, as instinctual as it is inevitable. It's a force that has driven human existence and evolution, compelling men to seek continuity and immortality through their offspring.

However, beyond cultural obligations and biological impulses lies a profound emotional dimension to the desire to become a father. This emotional aspect often manifests as a deep-seated yearning to nurture, educate, and form a lasting bond with one's children. The opportunity to shape a young life, to witness and contribute to the growth and development of a new generation, offers a sense of fulfillment and purpose unlike any other. The emotional journey of fatherhood, filled with love, challenges, and unparalleled rewards, is often cited by fathers as one of the most transformative experiences of their lives.

Moreover, the modern understanding of fatherhood has evolved to embrace more than the traditional role of a provider or a disciplinarian. Today, men increasingly recognize the importance of being emotionally available and actively involved in their children's lives. This shift reflects a growing understanding that the value of fatherhood lies not just in the biological act of procreation but in the lifelong commitment to nurturing and guiding another human being.

The motivations behind embracing fatherhood are as varied and complex as the men who choose to undertake this journey. Becoming a father is significant and life-changing, whether driven by cultural and religious beliefs, biological instincts, or emotional desires. It is a role that encompasses the responsibility of providing and protecting and the profound joy and fulfillment that comes from nurturing and shaping the future generation. Fatherhood, in all its facets, is a journey that fundamentally alters a man, reshaping his identity, his priorities, and his view of the world.

In this complex tapestry of motivations behind fatherhood, it is crucial to acknowledge that not all paths to fatherhood are intentional or planned. In some cases, men become fathers through unforeseen circumstances, including what some might perceive as mistakes or even instances of entrapment. These situations add another layer of complexity to understanding fatherhood and its motivations.

Instances where fatherhood results from unintended pregnancies can lead to a range of emotions and decisions. For some men, what initially appears as a mistake or an unplanned event transforms into accepting and embracing fatherhood. The unexpected journey into parenting can lead to profound personal growth and reevaluating priorities and values. These fathers often find that the unforeseen challenge of fatherhood becomes a defining and enriching experience.

However, there are also scenarios where men feel entrapped into fatherhood. This can occur in relationships where pregnancy is used to bind or manipulate, leaving men feeling trapped in a role they were not prepared for or did not choose. Such situations can lead to complicated emotional and interpersonal dynamics, impacting the father's relationship with the child and the other parent. In these cases, the journey to embracing fatherhood can be more tumultuous, marked by feelings of resentment, obligation, or conflict. And just because you don't know of this happening or have not witnessed it does not mean it does not occur. It may have happened to someone you know, and they have concealed it and suppressed all emotion and feeling about it.

It is essential to recognize that these less conventional routes to fatherhood still hold the potential for positive outcomes. Men who find themselves unexpectedly in the role of a father often rise to the occasion, developing strong bonds with their children and finding fulfillment in their parental role. The challenges and complexities of such situations can also lead to meaningful conversations and societal reflections on the nature of parenting, responsibility, and the support systems needed to assist fathers in successfully navigating these circumstances.

In summary, fatherhood encompasses a broad spectrum of experiences and motivations. While some men actively choose this path for cultural, biological, or emotional reasons, others find themselves in this role through less planned circumstances, including mistakes or entrapment. Regardless of the route to fatherhood, the role offers a unique opportunity for growth, challenge, and profound personal fulfillment. The journey of fatherhood, in all its forms, is an integral part of the human experience, shaping individuals and societies in multifaceted ways.

Another significant motivation for men to embrace fatherhood is their desire to break the cycle of fatherless homes—a pattern many might have experienced firsthand. Having grown up in homes without a father figure, these men often firmly commit to ensuring their children do not experience the same void. This decision is deeply rooted in their personal histories and the desire to provide a different, more positive experience for the next generation.

Men who grew up in fatherless homes understand the emotional and developmental gaps that can result from the absence of a father. Their personal experiences might include feelings of abandonment, challenges in forming stable relationships, or struggles with identity and self-worth. By choosing to be present and involved fathers, they seek to provide their children with the guidance, support, and emotional connection they might have missed.

This motivation goes beyond the personal; it's also about altering a familial pattern. Many of these men view fatherhood as an opportunity to end a cycle of absence and create a new legacy for their family. Many men want to be the first to be married and stay married, maintain that long-term commitment, and become a father who stays, no matter the circumstances. Their decision is often driven by a deep sense of racial and ethnic responsibility and a desire to rewrite the narrative of what it means to be a father within the black community and a black family's lineage. These men fulfill a personal desire and address a broader social issue of father-lessness by making this choice.

The impact of such a decision is significant for the individual family and society. Children who grow up with a dedicated father figure are often better equipped emotionally and socially, and they benefit from the diverse perspectives and experiences that an involved father brings to parenting. For society, these fathers are role models, demonstrating the positive effects of breaking negative family patterns and showing that the legacy of fatherlessness does not have to continue.

In conclusion, the decision to become a father, particularly for men who have experienced growing up in a fatherless home, is often driven by a powerful desire to provide their children with a different upbringing. These men are motivated by their past to create a new future, not just for their immediate family but as a contribution to a broader societal shift. This aspect of fatherhood highlights the role's transformative potential, not only in the lives of individuals but also in the fabric of communities and generations.

UNRAVELING THE INTRICACIES: THE INDISPENSABLE SCIENCE OF FATHERHOOD

Fatherhood, a journey that intertwines the threads of innate biological instincts and external environmental influences, presents a captivating fusion of nature and nurture. The timeless nature versus nurture debate takes on a new dimension when viewed through the lens of fatherhood. How much of fatherhood is driven by an inherent biological calling, and how much is sculpted by societal norms and personal experiences? This essay delves into the scientific viewpoints on fatherhood, drawing insights from genetics, psychology, and sociology to illuminate how men steer and fulfill their roles as fathers.

From the standpoint of genetics and biology, fatherhood can be seen as a natural, instinctual behavior. Biological predispositions may influence paternal instincts, suggesting that certain aspects of fatherhood are hardwired in a man's DNA. For instance, research in evolutionary biology proposes that the drive to protect and provide for one's offspring is a fundamental trait that evolved to ensure the survival and propagation of one's genes. Hormonal changes observed in new fathers, such as increased levels of oxytocin, also support the idea that certain aspects of fatherhood are biologically ingrained.

However, the role of nurture, or the influence of environment and upbringing, is equally significant in shaping fatherhood. Sociological studies have consistently demonstrated that cultural contexts and societal expectations are crucial in defining what it means to be a father. These studies suggest that many behaviors associated with fatherhood, including emotional involvement and parenting style, are primarily learned and influenced by societal norms. For example, the variations in fatherhood roles across different cultures and historical periods indicate that societal factors significantly affect how fatherhood is perceived and enacted.

Psychological research further illuminates how a man's upbringing and experiences shape his approach to fatherhood. Men with positive paternal figures often emulate these role models, while those who grew up without such figures might seek to provide a different experience for their children. Additionally, the psychological growth accompanying the transition to fatherhood, including the development of empathy, patience, and responsibility, highlights the transformative impact of environmental and relational factors.

In conclusion, the science of fatherhood is a dynamic field that straddles the boundaries of nature and nurture. While biological factors provide a foundational understanding of paternal instincts, environmental influences, cultural contexts, and personal experiences shape the journey into fatherhood. This complex interaction underscores that fatherhood is not merely a biological destiny but a role continuously molded by many external and internal forces. Understanding this interplay is critical to appreciating the depth and diversity of the paternal experience.

RELIGIOUS AND CULTURAL PERSPECTIVES ON FATHERHOOD

Fatherhood, a role as old as humanity itself, is deeply influenced by religious and cultural contexts. Across the globe, varying belief systems and cultural traditions paint a diverse picture of what it means to be a father. These perspectives shape individual experiences of fatherhood and inform societal expectations and values associated with the role. This essay explores how different religions and cultures perceive fatherhood, highlighting the myriad ways these belief systems and norms influence men in their journey as fathers.

Fatherhood is imbued with a sense of sacred duty in many religious contexts. For instance, Christianity often associates fatherhood with stewardship and moral leadership. The Christian doctrine emphasizes the father's role in guiding the family in faith and ethical values, drawing parallels with God's paternal nature. Similarly, in Islam, fatherhood is regarded as a responsibility bestowed by God, emphasizing the father's role in providing for the family not just materially but also spiritually and morally.

In Hinduism, the father's role is intricately linked with the concept of 'Dharma,' or righteous duty. Here, fatherhood extends beyond the biological connection to include the responsibilities of imparting wisdom, nurturing moral values, and ensuring the continuation of religious and cultural practices. In Jewish culture, fathers are central to the passing down traditions and teachings and play a crucial role in their children's spiritual education.

Culturally, the perception of fatherhood varies significantly across societies. In many traditional African cultures, for example, fathers are seen as the pillars of the family, providing not just economic support but also serving as the moral compass and link to ancestral heritage. In many Asian cultures, particularly those influenced by Confucianism, fathers are often viewed as figures of authority and respect, emphasizing filial piety.

In contrast, Western cultures, particularly in contemporary times, have seen a shift in the perception of fatherhood. The increasing emphasis on gender equality and shared parenting responsibilities has begun redefining fathers' traditional roles. The contemporary Western father is often expected to be more involved in direct childcare, challenging the conventional notion of the father as primarily a breadwinner.

Despite these varied perspectives, a common thread in many cultures and religions is the recognition of the father's role in providing stability, guidance, and love in the upbringing of children. Fathers are seen as crucial in the emotional and moral development of their offspring, regardless of the specific duties ascribed to them by their cultural or religious context.

In conclusion, the religious and cultural lenses through which fatherhood is viewed significantly influence how men approach and fulfill this role. These perspectives provide a rich tapestry of understanding, highlighting the diverse ways fatherhood is experienced and valued worldwide. They remind us that fatherhood, while universal in its presence, is profoundly shaped by each society's beliefs, traditions, and norms.

THE SOCIETAL IMPACT OF FATHERHOOD

Society's fabric is intricately woven with various threads, one of the most significant being the role of fathers. When men take an active and involved role in parenting, the benefits extend beyond the immediate family unit and permeate society. This essay explores the societal impact of fatherhood, drawing upon crucial insights from Michael E. Lamb's seminal work The Role of the Father in Child Development. Lamb comprehensively analyzes how a father's involvement shapes the child and society.

THE TRANSFORMATIVE ROLE OF FATHERS

Fathers play a pivotal role in their children's emotional, cognitive, and social development. Lamb's research highlights how involved fathers contribute to better educational outcomes for their children. Children with active fathers are likelier to perform well academically, exhibit higher concentration levels, and show greater problem-solving skills. Furthermore, fatherly involvement is linked to lower delinquency rates and antisocial behavior in children, contributing to a more stable and law-abiding society.

EMOTIONAL AND SOCIAL DEVELOPMENT

One of the key themes in Lamb's book is the transformative impact of fathers on the emotional development of children. Active fatherhood fosters emotional security and self-confidence, laying the foundation for a more emotionally balanced adulthood. Fathers often engage with their children in ways that challenge them, encouraging them to explore and take calculated risks, thereby developing resilience and adaptability. This nurturing of emotional intelligence in childhood paves the way for developing empathetic, understanding, and socially responsible adults.

THE RIPPLE EFFECT ON SOCIETY

The influence of active fatherhood extends beyond individual families, creating ripples throughout society. As Lamb points out, engaged and present fathers provide models of positive masculinity, redefining strength as a combination of care, responsibility, and emotional openness. This redefinition helps break down harmful stereotypes and promote gender equality in the home and the workplace.

Children who grow up with involved fathers are likelier to replicate this behavior in their adult lives, perpetuating a cycle of positive parenting practices. This cycle contributes to developing a more empathetic, responsible, and nurturing society. Additionally, the active role of fathers in household responsibilities supports women's empowerment, promoting a more balanced and equitable distribution of domestic duties and professional opportunities.

In conclusion, the societal impact of fatherhood, as comprehensively analyzed by Michael E. Lamb, is profound and multifaceted. Active and involved fathers contribute not only to the well-being and development of their children but also to creating a more balanced, empathetic, and responsible society. The presence of a caring, engaged father figure shapes the future in innumerable ways, from fostering emotional intelligence and academic success in children to challenging and reshaping societal norms. In essence, the role of fathers is indispensable in building a stronger, more cohesive society.

HOW CHILDREN LEARN

If a child lives with criticism, He learns to condemn.

If a child lives with hostility, He learns to fight.

If a child lives with ridicule, He learns to be shy.

If a child lives with shame, He learns to feel guilty.

If a child lives with tolerance, He learns to be patient.

If a child lives with encouragement, He learns confidence.

If a child lives with praise, He learns to appreciate.

If a child lives with fairness, He learns justice.

If a child lives with security, He learns to have faith.

If a child lives with approval, He learns to like himself.

If a child lives with acceptance, He learns to find love.

By Dorothy Lew Nolte

The foundational principle that Dorothy Lew Nolte's poem "Children Learn What They Live" encapsulates is the profound impact of the environment on child development. This poetic framework is not just a story but is underpinned by a wealth of psychological evidence. For instance, the poem begins with the line, "If a child lives with criticism, he learns to condemn." This aligns with the psychological theory of social learning, which declares that children adopt behaviors they observe. Albert Bandura's work on social learning theory suggests that children are active learners who assimilate behaviors through observation and imitation (Bandura, 1977). Children regularly exposed to criticism may internalize a critical worldview, often perpetuating a cycle of negativity.

Historical and sociological evidence further supports the environment's influence on learning. Sociological studies, such as those examining the effects of family dynamics on child development, reinforce the idea that children raised in hostile environments may be more inclined to engage in conflict (Eron et al., 1971). Hostility becomes a learned response, a survival mechanism in an antagonistic world.

Similarly, when the poem states, "If a child lives with ridicule, he learns to be shy," it reflects psychological findings on the development of self-concept. Ridicule can damage a child's emerging self-esteem, resulting in withdrawal and shyness as a defense mechanism (Harter, 2012). The developmental psychology literature emphasizes that consistent ridicule undermines a child's intrinsic sense of worth, often leading to a reticence to engage openly with others.

On a positive note, the poem suggests that living with encouragement and praise fosters confidence and appreciation. These assertions are mirrored in positive psychology, which has shown that positive reinforcement can enhance a child's self-efficacy and capacity for gratitude (Seligman et al., 2005). A child's environment, steeped in affirmation, lays the groundwork for internalizing positive traits and a healthy self-image.

Fairness and its impact on learning justice have been a cornerstone of societal development. Philosophers like John Rawls have articulated theories of justice that emphasize fairness as a fundamental virtue (Rawls, 1971). When children experience fairness, they learn to recognize and value justice, a principle crucial for developing ethical reasoning.

The poem states that security in a child's environment is also crucial for faith development. Erik Erikson's stages of psychosocial development highlight the importance of establishing trust in early childhood (Erikson, 1950). A secure environment fosters a sense of trust in the world, which can evolve into faith in oneself and others.

The poem's latter part reflects the importance of approval, acceptance, and friendship in nurturing self-like and love for the world. From a sociological perspective, the notion of "significant others" described by Herbert Mead underscores the role of social interactions in developing self-identity and the capacity for empathy (Mead, 1934).

The narrative then transitions into personal reflection, leveraging the poem's themes to provoke a "Fatherhood Inquisition." It challenges caregivers to examine the atmospheres they create, drawing parallels to the cultivation of plants—a rose cannot thrive among weeds. This metaphor highlights the need for a conducive environment for growth, echoing the call for positive reinforcement in developmental psychology. The chapter further delves into operant conditioning, a theory famously developed by B.F. Skinner posits that behavior is shaped by consequences (Skinner, 1938). It is not just about accountability, as the original text suggests, but also about understanding the nuances of reinforcement and punishment as tools for shaping behavior.

Moreover, the chapter concludes by emphasizing the transparency of parental actions. Children learn even when it seems they are not watching. This observation underscores the importance of modeling appropriate behavior, which stands at the core of social learning theory. In essence, the chapter could be further enriched by integrating these psychological, historical, and sociological perspectives to underscore the profound impact of the environment on child development. By creating a nurturing atmosphere, caregivers can foster the growth of children who are confident, just, and capable of love—both for themselves and the wider world.

Everyone reading this already knows that listening is an important skill for language and communication. Furthermore, as children grow between the ages of 3 and 5 (transitioning from single-channel attention, being able to control what they focus on, to a two-channel attention phase. Alternatively, what

I like to call multitasking with senses. It sounds better to say the child can attend to visual and audio cues together). This is when we need to pay attention to what we say, how, when and where we say it. So, we remind ourselves of Philippians 4:6-7 as it tells us that we must be careful for nothing, but in everything by prayer and supplication with thanksgiving let your requests be made known unto God. When children are around 5 years old, they are in a phase of fully integrated attention. They can carry out more complex tasks, focus on various-sized groups, ignore distractions and maintain their attention for a reasonable amount of time.

Therefore, fathers, mind your tongue and be careful about nothing as we monitor our speech at home, work, play, and with friends. Children did not discover gossip and foul language independently, and they did not learn how to lie either. If listening is a skill for the development of the child's language and communication, then what they hear from us, like affirmations of positivity, expressions of love and admiration for one another and ourselves, and the tones, pitches, and inflections of words in a conversation, that tell our mood and emotional state, for the words that you use, are the words they will use.

Moreover, what they hear shapes their behaviors and affects their mental health. What a child hears can become ingrained in their minds for years, no matter what it is. Words hurt, and words heal. Moreover, when your son listens, he receives information programming him and his future self. A significant part of that programming is how children learn by pestering us with questions. This is highly important, and busy, overwhelmed, overworked, underappreciated parents forget how much of our children's knowledge comes from us. Some of us have not accepted the idiom that says, "You cannot teach what you do not know. And you cannot lead where you will not go." children learn a great deal of information through three types of questions, and they ask many of them.

Children ask parents cognitive questions, which is how to seek new information and satisfy a curiosity. They ask social questions for interaction, draw attention for contact, and receive validation, especially from their father. When the operational questions come, we need to understand and see these as questions for help or permission. Furthermore, it is upon us as fathers to see that we cannot give any answer.

Moreover, we teach integrity, honor, and discipline in our answers. This is a part of leadership. By not teaching the children how to communicate and not answering their questions, we are mismanaging our family and setting them up to fail as we fall apart and fall behind as leaders.

Furthermore, you cannot lead from behind. We must do more than blurt out an answer to our children. We must do more with our thinking and expressions of love. That causes us to do more. Furthermore, the more we do, the more we encourage. Moreover, that encouragement creates confidence not just in them but in us also.

TO BE ONE HE HAS TO SEE ONE

WHAT ARE YOU SHOWING THEM?

The axiom "Do as I say, not as I do" is a paradox that fails to acknowledge the nature of human learning, especially in children. The developmental psychology literature is clear: children are adept at imitating behaviors observed in their caregivers. They often cannot discern which actions are appropriate to replicate (Bandura, 1977). This imitation extends beyond mere action into attitudes, beliefs, and problem-solving strategies. Children are not simply passive recipients of information but active constructors of understanding, picking up on their environment's overt and subtle cues (Gopnik et al., 1999).

The Bible says, "Train up a child in the way he should go; even when he is old, he will not depart from it" (Proverbs 22:6, ESV). The Islamic tradition also emphasizes the importance of role modeling in upbringing. Prophet Muhammad (PBUH) said, "Each of you is a shepherd, and each of you is responsible for his flock" (Sahih al-Bukhari, 6719), indicating the responsibility of adults to guide the young through example.

For a boy to understand what it means to be a man, he needs to observe the daily endeavors of a male role model or, as we say, a REAL model — traditionally, his Father. This observation is not limited to professional pursuits. However, it encompasses the totality of life, including personal discipline, moral conduct, and relational dynamics. In "Visions for Black Men," Dr. Na'im Akbar underscores the significance of men as builders — not just of structures but of character, community, and legacy (Akbar, 1991).

In the context of Dr. Na'im Akbar's work, the concept of men as builders extends beyond the physical construction of buildings to the more profound crafting of one's moral fiber, the shaping of community values, and the establishment of a lasting legacy. Building character involves consistently demonstrating honesty, resilience, and compassion. Building community refers to fostering a sense of unity, support, and shared purpose among a group of people. Building a legacy is about creating something that outlasts one's life, whether through positive impacts on others, achievements, or societal contributions that are remembered and valued by future generations.

Picture someone you know who volunteers his time to mentor young people in his neighborhood as an example of a builder. He lays the foundation for a supportive and interconnected community through his actions. He builds character within himself by committing to service and integrity, and he builds character in young people by serving as a role model. His guidance and wisdom helped shape the mentees' values and future behaviors, contributing to the community's social fabric.

Imagine a man who starts a community garden in an urban neighborhood that lacks green spaces. He collaborates with local families, schools, and businesses to cultivate the garden. He teaches children about responsibility and teamwork as they plant and care for the garden, thereby instilling values and building character. The garden becomes a hub for community interaction, education, and cooperation, strengthening communal bonds. Over time, the garden enriches the neighborhood ecologically and socially, becoming a part of a legacy.

To apply the principles of being a builder in real life, a man might begin with self-reflection to identify his core values and then strive to live by them daily, thereby building his character. He can engage with his community by participating in local events, supporting local businesses, and volunteering for causes that improve the quality of life for his neighbors. To build a legacy, he could focus on creating lasting change through initiatives that align with his values, like starting a scholarship fund, leading community enhancement projects, or advocating for critical social causes. The key is for the actions to have a meaningful and enduring impact that resonates with others and is a testament to his commitment and vision.

The Biblical scriptures in Proverbs reflect the wisdom of showing diligence and foresight, virtues that can be instilled through observation and participation. Proverbs 21:5

highlights the benefits of diligent planning. At the same time, Proverbs 24:27 advises preparation and groundwork as precursors to establishing one's house — literally and metaphorically. These principles resonate with the Islamic value of "tawakkul" — trusting God's plan after making one's effort (Quran 3:160).

The teachings of Proverbs about diligence and foresight, alongside the Islamic concept of "tawakkul," which means trusting in God after exerting one's effort, provide a holistic approach to life and parenting. Proverbs 21:5 emphasizes the rewards of careful planning and hard work.

At the same time, Proverbs 24:27 suggests that laying a solid foundation is crucial before building one's life (or house). Tawakkul, from an Islamic perspective, involves doing one's best and then trusting in God's plan, acknowledging that human effort is part of a larger divine tapestry.

Imagine a father who wants to teach his children the value of diligent planning and trust in God. He decides to start a family garden. He involves his children in every step - from selecting seeds to determining where each plant should go. He teaches them the importance of understanding the seasons, soil preparation, and regular maintenance. Despite their best efforts, a sudden storm damages part of their garden. He uses this opportunity to show his children how to rebuild and adapt their plans, emphasizing the need to trust in a more excellent plan and learn from every outcome.

The Father also plans for his children's education by practicing these principles. He researches schools, sets aside savings, and involves them in discussions about their interests and future goals, illustrating diligent planning. However, it also acknowledges uncertainties — like changing interests or unforeseen opportunities — reinforcing the concept of tawakkul. He openly discusses with his children that after doing their best, they must trust that things will unfold as they are meant to, according to God's plan. This approach helps his children understand the balance between personal effort and faith.

In this context, trusting in God means recognizing that while humans are responsible for planning and effort, the ultimate outcomes are not always within their control. This trust is shown by not being overly anxious about the future and accepting the consequences, especially those beyond one's control, with a calm and positive attitude. It involves prayer or meditation, seeking guidance and strength from a higher power while striving in the worldly sense.

To demonstrate this to children, a father can discuss his decisions, considering both practical aspects and spiritual guidance. He can share times when things did not go as planned yet led to unexpected, sometimes better, outcomes. By living a life that balances effort with faith, a father teaches his children to work hard, plan wisely, and ultimately surrender to the greater wisdom of God's plan, instilling in them a sense of peace and resilience in the face of life's unpredictabilities.

THE BABY IS WATCHING:

In light of the boundless creativity and imagination that define childhood, it becomes imperative for parents to be acutely aware of their influence on their children. In their formative years, children are exceptionally impressionable, often mirroring the behaviors, attitudes, and values they observe in their parents. This concept is rooted in the social learning theory articulated by psychologist Albert Bandura, which emphasizes that children learn and adopt behaviors through observing and imitating others, particularly those in parental roles (Bandura, 1977).

Playing, too, mimics the adult world. Through playing, children enact scenarios drawn from the behaviors they witness through sight and sound, movies and TV, music, and most importantly, YOU! These imaginative plays are a child's way of making sense of the world and their role in it (Vygotsky, 1967). Thus, a child must see constructive and positive behaviors modeled consistently.

Therefore, parents are responsible for modeling behaviors encouraging creativity, curiosity, and active engagement with the world. In an era increasingly dominated by technology, parents must judiciously manage their children's exposure to electronic devices. Research has shown that excessive screen time can impede developmental progress in children, affecting their attention span, creativity, and social skills (Twenge & Campbell, 2018). By delaying the introduction of cell phones and other electronics until children have reached an appropriate level of mental maturity and understanding, parents can help ensure that their children develop a healthy relationship with technology.

However, the impact of negative behaviors and prejudices cannot be understated. Both Christianity and Islam advocate for the purity of a child's heart and the danger of leading them astray. Matthew 18:6 warns of the severity of causing a child to stumble, while the Qur'an states, "O you who have believed, protect yourselves and your families from a Fire..." (Surah 66:6), implying the duty to shield children from harmful influences. We do not want to stop there; let's get deeper.

HARMFUL INFLUENCES & THEIR IMPACT:

Children are particularly susceptible to external influences in their formative years, making it crucial for parents to be vigilant about the types of propaganda and messages they are exposed to. Propaganda that glorifies ignorance, intolerance, or violence can have a profound impact on a child's developing psyche. Exposure to such content can negatively shape their attitudes, beliefs, and behaviors. For instance, media or social platforms celebrating ignorance may lead children to undervalue education, critical thinking, and informed decision-making. Similarly, content that subtly promotes intolerance or prejudice can instill harmful biases and attitudes in children, contributing to a divisive and intolerant society.

Instead, it is vital to foster an environment that celebrates and strengthens creativity. Engaging children in activities stimulating their imagination, like arts and crafts, storytelling, and outdoor play, contributes significantly to their cognitive and emotional development (Ginsburg, 2007). Such activities nurture creativity and promote physical health and social skills.

THE NATURE AND EFFECT OF PROPAGANDA:

Propaganda that mainly influences people to celebrate ignorance reinforces an idiot mentality and creates attraction to believe erroneous narratives are a grave danger. It frequently appeals to emotions rather than rational thought, making it especially appealing and digestible for younger minds still developing critical thinking skills. This content often presents complex issues in black-and-white terms, discouraging nuanced understanding and critical analysis. Regularly exposing children to such messaging can limit their ability to think critically, empathize with others, and understand the complexity of the world around them.

SUBLIMINAL MESSAGING AND THE SUBCONSCIOUS:

Subliminal messaging, a technique that transmits information below the threshold of human consciousness, can also significantly impact children. Although not consistently negative, it can subtly influence attitudes and behaviors when used in harmful ways. These messages are often delivered through visual or auditory stimuli. The subconscious mind processes them without the individual's conscious awareness. For children, whose brains are still developing and are more malleable, repeated exposure to particular subliminal messages can gradually shape their perceptions and beliefs. This subconscious programming can influence their choices, preferences, and attitudes long into adulthood.

PARENTS MITIGATING HARMFUL INFLUENCES:

Given the potential for harm, it is essential for parents to actively protect their children from propaganda that celebrates ignorance or harmful ideologies. This involves being aware of the content children are exposed to, including television shows, movies, internet content, and even conversations in their environment. Parents should engage in open discussions with their children about what they see and hear, helping them develop the critical thinking skills needed to analyze and question the information they encounter. By fostering an environment of curiosity, critical thinking, and open dialogue, parents can help their children develop a healthy skepticism towards misleading or harmful propaganda and learn to process information more discerning and thoughtfully. This active engagement is crucial to guiding children to become well-informed, empathetic, and thoughtful adults.

Moreover, combating laziness and fostering a culture of activity within the family is crucial. Family activities, whether outdoor adventures, sports, or collaborative projects, encourage a healthy lifestyle, strengthen family bonds, and provide practical settings for children to learn and imitate positive behaviors (Hofferth & Sandberg, 2001).

Parents play a pivotal role in shaping their children's development and perspectives. By being mindful of their actions, encouraging creative endeavors, carefully introducing technology, and promoting family activities, they can significantly influence their children's growth into imaginative, healthy, and well-rounded individuals. This approach is about protecting and nurturing a child's innate creativity and joy and setting a foundation for them to develop into capable, responsible, and innovative adults.

Additional References

- Bandura, A. (1977). *Social Learning Theory.* General Learning Press.

- Twenge, J. M., & Campbell, W. K. (2018). Associations between screen time and lower psychological well-being among children and adolescents: Evidence from a population-based study. *Preventive Medicine Reports, pp. 12,* 271–283.

- Ginsburg, K. R. (2007). Play is essential in promoting healthy child development and maintaining strong parent-child bonds. *Pediatrics, 119*(1), 182–191.

- Hofferth, S. L., & Sandberg, J. F. (2001). How American Children Spend Their Time. Journal of Marriage and Family, 63(2), 295-308.

THE POWER OF PATIENCE, RESILIENCE, AND RESOURCEFULNESS:

By demonstrating resilience and adaptive problem-solving in the face of adversity, a father shows his son that victory often comes after overcoming challenges. This echoes the

Islamic teaching that with hardship comes ease (Surah 94:5-6) and aligns with the Biblical understanding that "suffering produces perseverance; perseverance, character; and character, hope" (Romans 5:3-4, NIV).

Let's break this down to see what it looks like. Imagine a scenario where a father and son are building a model airplane together. It is a complex project that requires patience, precision, and much trial and error. As they begin assembling the pieces, they encounter a series of setbacks: parts do not fit together as expected, the instructions are confusing, and, at one point, a crucial piece snaps in half, seemingly ruining the project.

Instead of showing frustration or giving up, the Father takes a deep breath and assesses the situation. He finds a way to repair the broken piece with glue and improvised materials from around the house. When the instructions are unclear, he teaches his son how to seek out additional resources, finding a video online that provides a more precise demonstration. Each obstacle is met with calm deliberation and creative thinking.

The son observes his Father's unwavering commitment to solving each new problem as they work together. Despite the difficulties, his Father remains hopeful and resourceful, embodying the spirit of perseverance. After hours of meticulous effort, they finally completed the model airplane. The Father takes this moment to reflect with his son on the journey they have just undertaken, emphasizing that the satisfaction of their accomplishment is much sweeter because of the hurdles they overcame.

Through this experience, the son learns an invaluable life lesson about resilience. He understands that victory is not just about the final success but also about the growth and development that come from facing and conquering challenges. The Father has bonded with his son over a shared task and imparted wisdom that resonates with profound spiritual teachings. After every difficulty, there is relief, and it is through enduring hardship that one builds character and hope.

WHAT YOU SEE IS LOVE:

In relationships, a son witnessing his Father expressing love and respect toward his mother affects his understanding of the partnership and future interactions with women. The Bible speaks of husbands loving their wives as Christ loved the church (Ephesians 5:25). At the same time, the Hadith emphasizes kindness to women (Sahih Muslim, 1468). Witnessing a loving and equitable partnership can teach a child about mutual respect and the value of collaboration.

In exploring the profound impact of a father's behavior on his son's perception and understanding of relationships, particularly with women, it is essential to delve into the nuances of interpersonal dynamics and the REAL modeling in childhood development. The influence of a father's interaction with the mother in terms of love and respect serves as a critical blueprint for a son's future relationships and his overall approach to partnership and collaboration. We aim to unpack this concept by drawing on biblical and Islamic teachings as foundational references and to offer insights into how fathers can harness this understanding to enhance their role and, consequently, the developmental trajectory of their sons.

A wealth of psychological research supports the principle that a son's observation of his Father's treatment of his mother informs his understanding of partnerships. According to Bandura's social learning theory, children learn social behavior, such as interaction, norms, and relationships, through observation and imitation. This suggests that when a father consistently displays love and respect towards the children's mother, the son observes and internalizes these behaviors as a normative framework for future interactions.

In religious teachings, this concept finds resonance and reinforcement in Ephesians 5:25, which advocates for husbands to love their wives as Christ loved the church and underpins the idea of sacrificial and unconditional love. This verse promotes a nurturing, selfless, and elevating model of love, suggesting that a father's love for the mother should reflect these qualities. Similarly, in Islam, the Hadith recorded in Sahih Muslim (1468) emphasizes kindness towards women. This aligns with a broader understanding of respect and compassion, which are essential in healthy and balanced relationships.

For fathers seeking to use this information to improve their role and benefit their sons, the first step is to deliberately demonstrate love and respect in their relationships. This can manifest in various forms, such as verbal affirmations of love and appreciation, active listening, empathetic understanding, and equitable partnership in household and parenting responsibilities. By doing so, fathers create a harmonious home environment and set a living example for their sons.

Moreover, engaging in open discussions about relationships and respect can further reinforce these observations. Fathers can use teachable moments to explain why they value and respect their partners, giving their sons a verbal framework to accompany their comments. This helps build emotional intelligence and a deeper understanding of fostering healthy relationships.

This approach has many benefits. Sons who grow up witnessing and internalizing these values are more likely to develop into empathetic, respectful, and understanding partners. Research in developmental psychology indicates that children who observe positive relationship dynamics are more likely to replicate them in their adult relationships, leading to healthier and more fulfilling personal interactions.

In conclusion, the role of a father in modeling love, respect, and integrity within the family unit is of paramount importance, particularly in influencing his son's perception and conduct in future relationships. This responsibility, deeply rooted in both religious teachings and psychological theory, goes beyond mere advice; it is a living example that fathers set through their actions, attitudes, and behaviors. They demonstrate unwavering respect and love towards the mother, providing a tangible, powerful blueprint for their sons. Such a model enriches the immediate family dynamic and weaves a more substantial societal fabric, fostering individuals who can build and sustain healthy, respectful, and loving relationships.

We understand the curiosity and anticipation surrounding the father-daughter dynamics, and we assure you that this vital aspect has been noticed. A dedicated exploration of this relationship, enriched with insights and guidance, is forthcoming. However, our current focus on men and boys is deliberate and necessary. We are laying a cornerstone for broader societal change by addressing and reshaping their attitudes and behaviors. This journey is about equipping our sons with emotional tools, integrity, work ethic, and compassion, enabling them to function and operate life's intricacies with wisdom and moral strength. As we delve deeper into these crucial topics, we promise to provide valid information with the sincere intention to enrich and complete this essential conversation.

ADHD AN AUTHORS TESTIMONY

AIN'T NO DADDY AT HOME DISORDER

Under the glow of the sophisticated chandeliers of an upscale restaurant in LA, my family and friends indulged in a feast for the senses, surrounded by the plush opulence the City of Angels could provide. The establishment thrummed with life; each table was an island of laughter and dialogue, none more vibrant than ours. My brother-in-law at that time, who I considered a titan on the football field, and our companions, maestros of the film and music industry, were generously footing the bill, ensuring the evening was as carefree as it was sumptuous.

The air was electric with conversations that danced and weaved through the depths of innumerable topics, each a profound dive into the abyss of intellectual curiosity. It was as if every corner of a university's collective brainpower had concentrated around our table, engaging in discourse that sparked with the ferocity of untamed intellect. We volleyed from the existential musings of theology to the fantasy realms of DC & Marvel, navigated the philosophical currents of 'Star Wars' & 'Star Trek,' and traversed the expansive territories of world history, nutritional science, and sociology. Each subject was dissected and examined with an enthusiasm that was nothing short of biblical.

As we discussed relationships, sexuality, and gender roles more, the conversation became more serious. We started discussing parenting, which dramatically matters because of my past. My opinions stood out sharply and caused debate.

Back then, I was dealing with my past mistakes—I was an Army veteran who came home with a spirit partially broken, and my sense of patriotism diminished. The discipline, skills, and knowledge that I had honed in the military, once sources of pride and purpose, were now being misapplied in a life veering into criminal activity. This deviation from the path I once envisioned for myself was more than a divergence. I struggled to be a good person but often felt like the bad guy in my family. I thought I understood life, but it was like trying to hold water in my hands. I claimed to be wise but was often just as lost as anyone else. I was trying to improve myself based on society's expectations, even though I knew I wasn't following a perfect plan. I lived with this contradiction: I was self-centered, arrogant, and good at manipulating others.

As our conversation got deeper into parenting, fatherhood, and dating, my emphatic statement caught everyone's attention. Some of the women at our table stopped eating mid-bite, visibly surprised. Meanwhile, the men kept eating and chatting, but their attention subtly shifted towards the unfolding drama. A tense silence fell over our corner of the dining room. All eyes were on me; the women's faces were a mix of curiosity and suspicion, definitely thrown off by what I said and wondering what else I would say.

I remember this moment very clearly. I said, "I want my daughter to find happiness, date, and marry if she wishes. I prefer that she only deals with someone who's had a father in their life or at least a father's influence. I don't want her with a guy who didn't have that essential element in his life." The room fell silent, and I continued, "And for her friends, I wish for her to be surrounded by those from stable, loving two-parent households." My words seemed to echo, revealing an uncomfortable truth I've carried with me—a life shaped without a father's guidance. It was a candid confession of my deepest hope for my daughter to experience a different, more complete family dynamic than I did.

Suddenly, I was the focus of everyone's attention. The women present leaned in, their curiosity piqued, expecting a rational explanation or a sophisticated justification that might betray a sense of self-indulgence. I took a slow sip of my drink, the ice chiming in the glass, and felt the room's atmosphere thicken with unasked questions. A storm of silent scrutiny was brewing.

At that moment, I felt as though I had been whisked back to 1985, stepping right into an episode of "Voltron." My heart was a mix of childlike excitement and adult apprehension, reminiscent of watching the lions come together to form the legendary defender of the universe. The unity of the women around me, merging into a singular, inquisitive entity, mirrored the assembling of the five mighty lions, ready to confront

Hagar's RoBeast. With the same intensity that Voltron would face its foe, they directed a piercing, unified question my way: "What makes you say that?"

A side note. Reflecting on that moment now, it is still hard to fathom how a few of the women at that sitting would feel unnerved by what I said, seeing how several of them had fathers, came from stable two-parent households, have dated, are dating, and later married men cut from the same cloth. They are college graduates, and a few have at least attended a major university for more than two years and have thriving careers; some are still growing in theirs, and others have been retired by husbands or started other ventures that are proving to be a tremendous success in the right direction.

They also have children, and in their inner circles are, shall I say, "birds of a feather." I will admit that everything that glitters ain't gold, and what we see on the outside is not always the truth. However, the general results of having a father cannot be hidden. Whether a good man or not. Whether a peaceful household or not. We don't know everything happening behind closed doors. However, just like some women who have become major players in Hollywood, the showmanship and the illusion of the ideal "well-to-do Black upper class, started from the bottom now we here story" is awe-inspiring. Because they lived and are living currently, the words I uttered that evening. My apologies for rambling.

After I said my final words, I noticed that their disapproval was an incontestible wave, and no one seemed equipped to navigate the depths of my statement to find a strand of empathy or understanding. I braced myself, taking another sip of my drink, a small fortress of courage, before responding to defend my declaration. I used my life as the canvas, painting a vivid image with my words, "I know what it is to grow up without a father. And I understand the outcome all too well. Regardless of demographic or ethnicity, a boy without a father —or a child lacking the presence of strong, upstanding male figures—universally teeters on the brink. If not condemned to become a mere statistic, he skirts perilously close to the abyss of no return, viewed merely as only a number to certain sectors of society."

The silence that fell over the gathering became thick and heavy. I could almost see the cogs turning in their minds, questions forming like shadows in their eyes, my wife's included, which included the evil side eye signal to shut up. The din of other conversations enveloped us briefly, and then the probing began. But we decided to bookmark the discussion, close out our tab, and lift our glasses for one final toast, deferring our philosophical duel to another day, perhaps when spirits would guide us to a more enlightened discourse.

The conversation continued into the next day, and the numbers dwindled to a close-knit circle, forging an atmosphere ripe for raw honesty. In the warm afterglow of a lingering dinner party, my earlier proclamation became the center of more intense scrutiny, sparking fresh inquiries.

As I continued, supported by statistics from the late '90s to 2002 and the vivid hues of my narrative, I painted a picture of a landscape where children from single-parent households grapple with the allure of sexual encounters, mental health issues and much more. I was being transparent, as it was my story of many topics that disrespected me and my mother and the problems with academics, structure, and discipline. I also came close to becoming a teen father. That experience left its mark on me, as painful as a scorpion's sting. It was a narrow escape that nearly happened again, highlighting the harsh reality that children of single mothers in poverty often face and the likelihood of boys repeating mistakes they haven't learned from.

Growing up, I often felt down and surprisingly guilt-free, which led me to many careless adventures due to what is now understood as my low self-esteem and lack of focus. Without a father, my childhood was full of warning signs:

· Anger

· The potential for abuse

· A deep-seated crisis of self-belief

· The stereotype of the "angry black man" hanging over my future

My efforts at love often failed. It wasn't that I lacked courtesy —my mother ensured that. But around me, I saw no examples of what it meant to be a good man. The men my mother dated and those in our neighborhood reinforced a pattern of absent fathers and strained relationships. And even these men who had children my age, older and younger, didn't display what was essential for me to see. To be one, I needed to see one.

To me, chivalry was twisted, used by men to buy temporary love, a distorted show of respect. My real lessons in love were on the streets, in a few books and movies, and in calm moments with smut magazines, and with girls just as confused as I was. I didn't understand the dance of relationships, often finding myself moving off-beat and out of sync, just straight clueless, the "nice guy" who got taken advantage of.

School was a blur in my memory, clouded by any drug or drink I could get my hands on when adults weren't watching. Sports were my only bright spot, the one area where I excelled. However, real-life lessons were missing from my education, religion wasn't enough, and those shepherds of flocks were out-of-touch, old, biased, and disconnected. I was resolved not to let my daughter experience this same gap. I was determined to give her more.

That weekend, as I spoke about my past, it was a release and a deep dive into that earlier portion of my history, a story worthy of a book or a movie. Twenty-plus years later, the lessons from that night still resonate, surfacing in quiet moments of thought before finding their way into a journal and now onto this page.

My daughter's relationship with a young man raised by a strong father figure brought into focus the interplay between generations in our family. Our post-dinner conversation wove together the past and present, acknowledging the challenges of ADHD, humorously dubbed as 'Ain't No Daddy at Home Disorder,' a term I borrowed from Dr. Umar Ifatunde (Umar

Johnson). This light-hearted label belies the more profound sadness of my fatherless upbringing, despite the rich tapestry of love and support from the women in my family, from my mother's affection to my grandmother's nurturing and my aunts' robust presence. Reflecting on these experiences, I recognized the absence and the abundance in my life's story.

Although my father was absent, I tried to find my way, much like trying to navigate a maze without help. His fame as a top NFL receiver—selected in the first round and the fourth pick—cast a shadow over us. Yet, to me, he was barely more than a name and a fading story. I lacked the personal memories that would have shown me who my father was. He was supposed to be my favorite guy, my hero. Instead, he became a figure wrapped in bitterness and mystery, leaving me with a confusing blend of admiration and anger.

Watching my older and younger brothers play college football on TV in the '90s filled me with pride. Our family was known for athletics, tracing back to our father's success. However, our experiences differed considerably. They grew up with him, learning from his presence and guidance despite it not always being perfect. They had the opportunities I longed for. As I watched their lives and his from a distance, I believed that if I'd had the same support, if he had been there for me, my sports journey in high school and college would have been different. I played basketball, football, and baseball. I wrestled, boxed, and ran track but struggled to remain eligible for the critical moments I attribute to needing his guidance.

Yet, it would be unjust to overlook the orchestra of strong women who composed the symphony of my upbringing. My mother's unrelenting spirit, the grand matriarchs whose wisdom was as inexhaustible as their love, and the battalion of aunts who doubled as community sentinels—these were my champions. They were the ones who divided their time between church, work, grocery aisles, and the living room where soap operas whispered tales of drama and persistence. Their lives were portraits of independence and generosity, constantly extending a helping hand to the children of others while their own stood by their side. They were the architects of my happiest memories, for which I am grateful. Still, in the quiet recesses of my heart, where boyish dreams echo, the yearning for my father persists.

I dreamt of more than just passing moments, of something beyond the fleeting glimpses when he'd drift through town, always just beyond my grasp. Growing up, I believed that his absence was a measure of my worth; if only I sparkled a little brighter, I could seize his gaze and make him stay. Driven by a hunger for his nod of approval, I pushed myself to extremes. My training became my obsession. I rose to the top in sports, but each victory was laced with the bitterness of his neglect and my acts of self-sabotage. It was a fallacy I believed because I didn't know enough or understand what he was going through and what heavy burdens and demons he was at war with.

My relentless efforts echoed the fleeting male presence in my life—those temporary figures who came and went. They were mere phantoms in a play that never had a part for my father. We all shared a lot since that night at the dinner party.

As we laughed and shared stories over the weekend, I felt this was part of my healing. Each chuckle and shared memory wove into the fabric of a life beautifully pieced together in the love that stayed when my father didn't. It's a victory story that rises above the shadow of "Ain't no Daddy at Home Disorder," painted with the vibrant colors of love that filled his empty spaces.

Without a father, I felt lost in a world where authority and discipline didn't make sense, especially at school. The value of education was like a puzzle I couldn't solve; its pieces were always just out of reach. I drifted through school, disconnected, like the worn-out pages of a textbook that seemed to hold nothing for me.

I found a mentorship on the baseball field under the evening floodlights. Coach Mutcher, who looked a bit like me, unknowingly became a stabilizing presence in my life. My friendship with his son brought us closer, but this bond was limited to the confines of the baseball diamond. Another guiding light was the father of my cousins, Jamie and Jeremy, and a close friend of my father, Webb, who played in the league with my Pops. Then there was Atkinson and Coach Mixon, two men who inspired me as my coach to become a coach. These were coaches of mine for a time. I regretfully acknowledge that I squandered this golden opportunity because they cared and poured into me, but I was oblivious and didn't understand.

However, my experience with other coaches during my youth and high school years was different. These coaches, who didn't resemble me in appearance or background, praised my athletic skills but rarely guided me. They celebrated my sports achievements, which contributed to their team's successes, but they didn't offer the personal support or guidance I needed. To them, my value lies in the scores I can make, not in my aspirations or personal growth.

I longed for a father figure, a yearning that went unanswered. I reflect on how my aunts stepped in, teaching me to throw a football with a perfect spiral and master a quarterback's precise movements. They were my guides, showing me how to tie a Windsor knot from what they learned watching flickering images of an old VCR tutorial. At church, while other boys wore clip-on ties, mine was meticulously knotted—a silent testament to my unique upbringing. I found more father figures in women in the communities I grew up in than men who actually should have been the most qualified to do so.

Growing up, I didn't think much of learning life's lessons from the women in my life. Now, I understand the gap left by the lack of a traditional male role model was deeply felt, though it takes nothing away from the women who raised me. I learned to ride a bike through trial and error. When it came to standing up to bullies, my aunts stepped in, not because they wanted to, but because they had to. They taught me to throw a punch with the same reluctance.

Then there was Alonzo Latimore, or 'Pops' as we called him (RIP). His presence in my life was inconsistent, mirroring the ups and downs of his challenges, marked by stints in jail and periodic appearances in our home. Pops was the one who introduced me to boxing, teaching me the value of fighting with heart and determination. However, his guidance could have been more consistent with his presence. Amidst all this, I held onto the hope that my real father would someday enter my life, a man filled with wisdom to soothe my restless thoughts, insights to resolve my internal struggles, and answers to the questions that troubled my nights.

The women in my life rose to the occasion, gracefully bridging gaps, yet a part of my heart longed for a father's guidance—a heritage traditionally passed from father to son. Their resilience is admirable and a poignant reminder of what was lacking, a dual force that influenced my formative years. We are shaped by our environment, by the visible and the audible, by both the presence and the absence around us. We become reflections of these elements, silently molded by what is observed and what goes unnoticed. This unseen influence has quietly shaped me, as it has for many others.

We reflect the world we inhabit, absorbing and echoing what we hear and resonate with what we feel, quietly shaped by the unexamined influences that surround us. We latch onto role models and icons, drawn magnetically to those who stir something within us. My idols? They were not the traditional heroes but rather the pimps of the city streets and the charismatic villains of the screen. I found a kinship with the outcasts, the underdogs sculpted by unforgiving circumstances thrust into roles they did not choose but played with a defiant mastery.

I dove into the depths of history, seeking truth in the shadows of American and global events through movies, news, and books. The additional tales of misunderstood creatures like Frankenstein and the layered lives of Marvel's heroes—Silver Surfer, Hulk, Iron Man, Black Panther, Dr. Doom—stirred something in me. The X-Men and Morlocks' struggles and alliances struck a chord deep within my soul.

As a child, I was a master of masks, adept at manipulation, and a young politician in the making. I shifted shapes from school to home, from playgrounds to family feasts, leading with a self-serving cunning inspired by cinematic villains and, at times, by the rousing rhetoric of icons like Martin Luther King and Malcolm X.

But my path was paved with darkness—bullying, theft, cheating, gambling. Now, as a father, I see the scars of my past, and the path to redemption seemed like a maze without an exit. I once believed marriage would be the charm to right my wrongs, but I was wrong. The weight of my history is heavy, a reminder that change is no simple spell.

Fatherhood became an education through a litany of errors. My parenting was a tumultuous tide, creating and resolving chaos in endless cycles. The lack of control proved most daunting—a harrowing truth I was compelled to confront. I was not the captain of my ship, as I once believed. I was a player in a domestic masquerade, not the committed partner and leader my family deserved. Realizing my limitations was humbling, and my pride became my greatest adversary. Admitting this and seeking help was the challenge I was least prepared for, yet it was what I needed most.

I am the man I am today because I've overcome challenges and reached heights I never thought possible. My successes are built on the back of my failures. As a father standing on shaky ground, I've been broken and have cried out for help. This wasn't a weakness but a desperate desire to see my children—born from 1992 to 2001—surpass me in every way imaginable.

I was determined not to let my daughters suffer as their mothers did because of me. I couldn't stand the thought of my sons repeating my mistakes, attracting criticism, or struggling in their relationships because of unchecked flaws that might mark them as less than worthy in the eyes of the world. These fears haunted me because my father was a mystery; his life and lessons were elusive shadows in my life until we reunited on my 33rd birthday, and even that day was a stress and strain.

Driven to change, I sought guidance and a new path worth dedicating my life to. I worked to become the man I wanted to be—the man my family needed and deserved. And yes, I still stumble and struggle. But years ago, I realized that my children, growing up in a digital world, needed a different approach than what was used for a child in 1973. I had to evolve, not just for them, but for myself and the future of my bloodline and our community.

My realization changed everything. I transformed, learning that what I saw as my children's bad behavior was their way of coping with the world's complexities. Seeing through their eyes, I chose understanding over frustration. Parenting became about nurturing resilience, not enforcing rules.

Why scold a child for an accidental spill when I am not perfect and have unintentional spills? Why foster a home of fear instead of one filled with courage and growth? My roles as a father, coach, and entrepreneur merged, teaching me that as business and sports require strategy and foresight, so does fatherhood.

Having grown up without a father, I faced many trials but also triumphs that taught me resilience and wisdom. Fatherhood, like any great endeavor, is not something you master from the start—it is an art that flourishes with patience and the will to grow once you wholeheartedly commit to the journey. In this path, every experience, whether challenging or joyous, becomes a valuable lesson, shaping not just the father you become but also the individual you are. This journey of fatherhood, marked by its unique blend of responsibilities and rewards, requires continuous learning and adapting.

The absence of a father figure in my upbringing was a significant factor in my life, yet it did not define my capability to be a good father. Instead, it provided a unique perspective on the importance and impact of a father's role. I learned to find guidance and inspiration from various sources – mentors, role models, and the collective wisdom of the community around me. Their insights and my personal experiences helped me understand what it means to be a supportive, nurturing, and present father.

Over time, I have realized that fatherhood is not just about providing and protecting. It's about emotional presence, understanding, and fostering a deep connection with your children. It's about celebrating their achievements, big or small, and standing beside them through their struggles, offering encouragement and support. It's about teaching them, not just through words but through actions, the values of kindness, integrity, and perseverance.

Moreover, fatherhood has been a journey of self-discovery. It has taught me patience, empathy, and the power of unconditional love. The lessons learned from my past hardships have been instrumental in helping me guide and nurture my children and prepare them for their journeys. I have found a profound sense of purpose and joy in embracing fatherhood.

To those stepping into this journey, remember that while the path of fatherhood may be uncharted and challenging, it is enriching. Every father's journey is unique, and the willingness to embrace it, with all its uncertainties and learning curves, truly defines fatherhood. It's about growing alongside your children and, in the process, often rediscovering the world through their eyes. So, cherish each moment, learn from each experience, and continue to evolve as a father and a Man.

Indeed, the journey of fatherhood is an uncharted odyssey, devoid of any playbook, blueprint, or instructional guide. It's a venture where you navigate with the compass of your heart, charting a course through the unpredictable seas of parenting. You draw upon what you've seen, the wisdom you've gathered, and the instincts deep within you, but even then, it's a path where the map is constantly redrawn, each day a new lesson, each moment a fresh opportunity for growth.

As fathers, we embark on this journey armed with hope and love, yet the weight of our responsibility humbles us. We face setbacks, moments of doubt, and regrets that echo in the stillness of the night. We act, often driven by a fierce, protective love, our decisions colored by the fear of the unknown, the desire to shield and guide. Though rooted in the purest intentions, these actions might be misinterpreted as overbearing, stern, or unkind. But beneath this, perceived sternness beats a heart overflowing with immeasurable love, a love so profound and consuming that it can sometimes overwhelm both the giver and the receiver.

Our hearts must be seen and understood, brimming with unspoken dreams and silent sacrifices. It's not just the guardian of our deepest fears but also the sanctuary of our greatest hopes. In the depths of our eyes, our children must see the reflection of our soul, the unwavering commitment, the unyielding dedication. They must glimpse the tumultuous yet exhilarating journey of our spirit, marked by an unconditional love that knows no bounds, conditions, or reservations. They must see our heart of hearts.

We traverse this path not as flawless beings but as men learning, growing, and evolving with every step. We are sculptors, shaping not just our children's lives but also refining our essence, chiseling away at our imperfections, which also shapes our community, believe it or not. We discover our true strength, resilience, and capacity for boundless love in the crucible of fatherhood.

Ultimately, fatherhood is not just about raising children; it's about rising to the occasion, moment by moment, day by day. It's about being a beacon of hope, a bastion of safety, and a fountain of wisdom. It's about showing up, wholly and authentically, and embracing this journey with all its vicissitudes, with a heart wide open to the transformative power of love. This is our odyssey, our legacy, a testament to the indomitable spirit of fatherhood.

Remaining stagnant in parenthood is the only failure. Embracing change is a brave choice, the core of what it means to be a father.

THE JOURNEY OF FATHERHOOD: AN AUTHORS REFLECTION

Embracing the role of a father is a formidable journey, one that I embarked upon without any prior expertise. Over time, I have cultivated a deep comprehension of the responsibilities inherent in fatherhood. Navigating the intricacies of what it means to be a father and a man often feels akin to unraveling the complexities of the Da Vinci Code; the interpretation is subjective, varied across cultures, and deeply personal.

Fatherhood is not monolithic; it is nuanced and influenced by one's cultural background, religious doctrines, and the social environment. It embodies the pinnacle of adaptive creativity, as fathers must ingeniously address the unique challenges that arise within their families.

My quest to understand my role within the family unit has occasionally been clarified. Guidance on fatherhood is abundant and contradictory, with varying sources suggesting different approaches. For me, the key has been to assimilate this wealth of information and make informed decisions tailored to my family's specific needs.

Research substantiates the idea that there isn't a one-size-fits-all approach to parenting. A study by the Pew Research Center shows that views on parenting styles and values are vastly different across cultures and even within the same society (Pew Research Center, 2020). Furthermore, psychologists like Dr. Michael Thompson, co-author of "Raising Cain," emphasize the significance of fathers in developing a child's emotional health, underscoring that each father-child relationship will be unique (Thompson, 2009).

It is crucial to recognize that no philosopher, doctor, psychiatrist, faith leader, or therapist can fully anticipate the multitude of situations a father may encounter. This realization has impressed upon me the importance of pursuing knowledge in leadership and management fervently. By studying these disciplines, I am better equipped to steer my household and personal life with greater confidence and effectiveness.

Also, fatherhood is a dynamic and ever-evolving role that demands a father's full engagement, a willingness to learn, and the flexibility to adapt strategies as circumstances change. While there is no universal roadmap for the perfect way to father, informed and mindful parenting, grounded in love and understanding, is the cornerstone of successful fatherhood."

I wouldn't trade my current circumstances for anything in the world. The profound and unforeseeable personal growth I've experienced since becoming a father has expanded and transformed my perspective in countless ways. I take pride in the respect I receive from family, friends, the broader community, and particularly from other men for fulfilling my role as a father and parent.

Reflecting on my childhood, the absence of my father stands out as a significant hardship, one I only fully recognized upon introspection—what I describe as "taking off the blinders." My mother, a paragon of strength, immersed me in activities that often masked the void left by my father's absence. It was a dreary contrast to witness the dynamic of my childhood friend whose father was a constant presence, engaging us in football games, constructing soapbox cars, practicing boxing, and involving me in weekend projects.

The intermittent appearances of my own father seemed normal at the time; I didn't grasp the full impact until he ceased showing up altogether. The painful memories of unfulfilled promises—packed bags and unreturned calls—are etched in my memory, an emotional wound that, despite everything, has not diminished my love for him. Conversations with him today reveal the same pattern: more promises, little follow-through.

I've understood that a man's actual change must come from within, driven by a personal desire rather than external forces. This insight propels me to be exponentially better than my father. This ambition fills me with immense satisfaction when my son expresses gratitude for my presence. To me, the role of a father holds a divine quality, echoing the biblical notion of man being created in God's image.

Fatherhood is a continuous learning journey. Every day, I gain insights into my children, wife, and myself, developing patience and fortitude. The biblical reference that man was made in the image of God influences my self-development. I must continually educate myself to be prepared for the unexpected challenges that test me in all aspects of life.

I see myself not as a role model but as a "real model," speaking from lived experiences rather than theoretical knowledge. Many people discuss fatherhood hypothetically, never having endured the actual trials and mental strains it entails. A recent quote resonated: "If we want to see change in the world, we must be the change we wish to see." This quote catalyzed the writing of this book, offering guidance and inspiration to sons and young men growing up without paternal figures.

The importance of setting an example cannot be overstated; children are always observing, and we must embody it to foster improvement. This book is more than just a resource—it's a beacon of hope and a testament to the transformative power of engaged fatherhood. It's crafted not only to inform but also to excite young men about the journey of personal growth that lies ahead.

RELEVANT RESOURCES

I am asking this question out of curiosity and random thoughts: Who decides our role as fathers—us as men, women, children, society, or our cultures?

The role of fathers, or fatherhood, is influenced and shaped by a combination of factors, including personal choice, societal norms, cultural expectations, and the dynamics within individual families. A father's role is not determined by a single entity but is a complex interplay of personal choices, societal norms, cultural expectations, and family dynamics. Essentially, it's a collaborative decision influenced by multiple factors.

HERE IS A CLOSER LOOK AT EACH OF THESE INFLUENTIAL FACTORS:

Personal Choice (Men themselves): Ultimately, an individual man decides how he will perform his role as a father. This includes his level of involvement, the values he wants to impart, and how he balances fatherhood with other aspects of his life. Personal beliefs, ethics, and priorities are significant in these decisions.

Societal Norms: Society at large has expectations and norms regarding a father's role. These norms have evolved and continue to do so. In many modern societies, there is a growing emphasis on fathers being more emotionally available and involved in their children's lives compared to past generations, when the father's role was often primarily seen as a provider and disciplinarian.

Cultural Expectations: Different cultures have varying expectations for fathers. In some cultures, the father's traditional role as the primary breadwinner and disciplinarian is still prevalent. In contrast, in others, fathers are strongly encouraged to be actively involved in all aspects of child-rearing. Cultural beliefs and traditions can significantly influence how a man perceives and performs his role as a father.

Family Dynamics: Family dynamics, including the relationship with the child's other parent and the needs of the children, can significantly influence a father's role. For example, in a single-parent family, a father might have to take on a broader range of responsibilities. In other cases, the division of responsibilities and roles between parents can be influenced by factors such as each parent's work schedule, skills and interests, and approach to parenting.

Children's Expectations and Needs: Children can shape their father's role through their expectations and needs. A father might adapt his role based on each child's unique personality, interests, and needs.

Influence of Extended Family and Community: The extended family and community can also impact a father, offering models, expectations, and sometimes pressure regarding how he should act.

Economic and Social Conditions: Broader economic and social conditions, such as the availability of paternity leave, workplace policies, and societal attitudes toward gender roles, also significantly define fatherhood.

A father's role is not determined by a single factor. Instead, it is a dynamic interplay of personal choices, societal and cultural influences, family dynamics, and children's evolving needs and expectations. Fathers today often navigate a complex landscape as they seek to define and fulfill their role in a way that aligns with their values, their children's needs, and the expectations of their society and culture.

Various resources can be consulted to support and further explore the multiple influences on fathers' roles. These include academic research, books, articles, and organizations focused on parenting and fatherhood. Below are some resources that can provide more insight and information:

ORGANIZATIONS

National Fatherhood Initiative (NFI): This organization provides resources and researches the importance of a father's role in the family.

Fathers.com: Sponsored by the National Center for Fathering, this website offers articles, tips, and resources for fathers.

ONLINE ARTICLES AND BLOGS

Websites like Psychology Today, The Good Men Project, and HuffPost Parents often feature articles about fatherhood that discuss contemporary issues and perspectives.

GOVERNMENT AND EDUCATIONAL RESOURCES:

· Many government websites offer resources and information about parenting and fatherhood. For example, the U.S. Department of Health & Human Services has resources for fathers.

· Universities often publish studies and articles about family dynamics and parenting through their psychology, sociology, or family studies departments.

· Universities are pivotal in advancing our understanding of family dynamics, parenting, and the sociological and psychological aspects that underpin them. Many institutions around the globe conduct cutting-edge research and produce influential studies that contribute to our knowledge in these areas. Below is a list of universities known for their contributions through their psychology, sociology, or family studies departments.

THE UNITED STATES

Harvard University: Harvard's Department of Psychology and Graduate School of Education frequently publish research on child development, parenting practices, and family dynamics.

University of California, Berkeley: UC Berkeley's Department of Psychology and the Institute of Human Development are renowned for their developmental psychology and family studies research.

Stanford University: The Stanford Center on Longevity and the Department of Psychology offer insights into family dynamics, parenting, and the psychological aspects of family life.

University of Michigan: The University of Michigan's Department of Sociology and the Institute for Social Research are leading centers for research on family structures, parenting, and child welfare.

University of Minnesota: Home to the Institute of Child Development and the Department of Family Social Science, the University of Minnesota is a critical player in family studies research.

UNITED KINGDOM

University of Oxford: The Department of Social Policy and Intervention and the Oxford Centre for Family Law and Policy (OXFLAP) are notable for their research on family law, policy, and dynamics.

University College London (UCL): UCL's Institute of Education offers extensive research in child development, education, and family psychology.

CANADA

University of Toronto: The Department of Applied Psychology and Human Development and the Factor-Inwentash Faculty of Social Work at the University of Toronto are significant contributors to parenting and family dynamics research.

McGill University: McGill's Department of Educational and Counselling Psychology often publishes works on family therapy, child development, and parenting.

AUSTRALIA

University of Melbourne: The Melbourne Graduate School of Education and the Department of Social Work conduct research on family relationships, parenting, and education.

University of Sydney: The University of Sydney's School of Psychology and the Department of Gender and Cultural Studies offer diverse research insights into family dynamics and parenting.

EUROPE

University of Amsterdam (Netherlands): The Research Institute of Child Development and Education focuses on parenting, child psychology, and education.

University of Cambridge (UK): The Centre for Family Research is dedicated to studies on child development, parenting, and family psychology.

These universities and their respective departments and institutes are at the forefront of research that helps shape public policy, educational programs, and therapeutic practices related to family dynamics and parenting worldwide. Their contributions are essential for professionals in these fields and anyone interested in understanding the complex nature of family and parenting in contemporary society.

SOCIAL MEDIA AND ONLINE FORUMS:

Platforms like Reddit, Facebook groups, and other online communities for fathers can provide insight into dads' real-life experiences and perspectives today.

Reddit Communities

r/daddit: It is a popular subreddit for dads to share their successes, challenges, and humorous moments of fatherhood. It's a supportive space for fathers of any stage, from expecting to experienced dads.

r/predaddit: Designed explicitly for expectant fathers, this subreddit allows men to discuss the anticipation, preparation, and anxiety of becoming a dad for the first time.

r/SingleDads: This community focuses on the unique experiences of single fathers, offering a place for sharing advice, support, and stories about raising children alone.

r/DadForMinute: Users can seek fatherly advice, share victories, or offer support. It's a heartwarming space for those who may not have a father figure.

r/Fatherhood: A general subreddit for discussing all aspects of fatherhood, from newborn care to teenage dilemmas and everything in between.

Facebook Groups

The Dad's Edge - Alliance: This group offers a place for dads to discuss fatherhood, marriage, finance, and health, promoting personal growth and strong family bonds.

Dads With Daughters by Fathering Together: Fathers of daughters can join this group to share their experiences, ask for advice, and discuss the unique aspects of raising girls.

Rebel Dads: The Stay-at-Home Dad Network: Targeting stay-at-home dads, this group provides a platform for sharing the day-to-day experiences of father-led parenting, offering both light-hearted content and practical advice.

At-Home Dad Network: This community is for dads who are their families' primary caregivers. It focuses on exchanging tips, stories, and support for navigating at-home parenthood.

Other Online Communities

Fatherly Forum: This forum, hosted by the parenting resource website Fatherly, offers articles, advice, and community discussions on various aspects of modern fatherhood.

City Dads Group: This network of meetups and online forums across the United States is designed to connect dads in local areas for in-person gatherings, playdates, and father-focused discussions.

National At-Home Dad Network: Although primarily known for its annual convention, it offers an online community through its website and social media. It supports at-home dads by providing resources, networking opportunities, and advocacy.

Each platform is a valuable resource for fathers looking to connect with others with similar experiences and challenges. Whether seeking advice, sharing success stories, or looking for a laugh, dads of all backgrounds can find community and support through these online spaces.

DOCUMENTARIES AND PODCASTS

Numerous documentaries and podcasts explore fatherhood from various cultural, social, and personal perspectives, offering in-depth looks at the challenges and joys of fatherhood.

Documentaries

"Dads" (2019): Directed by Bryce Dallas Howard, this documentary features six fathers from around the world and explores the complexities of modern fatherhood. It combines humorous and heartfelt interviews with famous dads like Will Smith, Neil Patrick Harris, and Ken Jeong.

"The Evolution of Dad" (2010) This documentary examines how fatherhood has evolved, particularly in response to changing societal norms. It looks at the growing trend of stay-at-home dads and fathers actively involved in their children's lives.

"Father Soldier Son" (2020) Released by Netflix, this documentary follows a military family over ten years, offering a poignant look at the impact of service, sacrifice, and resilience on fatherhood and the bonds between a father and his sons.

"Daddy Don't Go" (2015) is a documentary that portrays the lives of four disadvantaged men in New York City as they struggle against the odds to be present and provide for their children. It challenges the stereotypes of absentee fathers in low-income communities.

"In My Father's House" (2015) This film follows the Grammy-winning rapper Che "Rhymefest" Smith as he seeks to reconnect with his homeless father. It explores themes of forgiveness, legacy, and the quest to understand one's identity in the shadow of paternal relationships.

Podcasts

"The Dad Edge Podcast" (formerly "The Good Dad Project") is a podcast Hosted by Larry Hagner that offers actionable advice to help men become their best fathers. It covers topics such as marriage, mental toughness, and fatherhood's challenges.

"Fatherly Podcast": Presented by the popular parenting resource Fatherly, this podcast explores the challenges of modern fatherhood. It features conversations with celebrities, experts, and everyday dads about how to be a better father.

"Dad's Unplugged" is a podcast Tailored for dads looking for support and community. It tackles various aspects of parenting from a dad's perspective, offering insights into balancing work, family life, and personal growth.

"Modern Dadhood" is an ongoing conversation about the joys, challenges, and general insanity of being a dad today. The podcast mixes interviews, storytelling, and music to create a uniquely engaging listening experience.

"Paternal" is a podcast featuring in-depth conversations about manhood and fatherhood and the challenges men face to become better fathers and men.

These documentaries and podcasts provide:

- Valuable insights into the nuanced experiences of fathers across the globe.

- Reflecting on the universal themes of love and responsibility.

- The transformative journey of fatherhood.

They are powerful resources for anyone looking to understand the depth and diversity of paternal experiences.

CULTURAL AND SOCIOLOGICAL TEXTS

Books and papers that delve into the cultural and sociological aspects of parenting and gender roles can offer a deeper understanding of how societal norms and cultural practices influence fatherhood.

Books

"Fatherhood: Evolution and Human Paternal Behavior" by Peter B. Gray and Kermyt G. Anderson provides an evolutionary perspective on fatherhood. It examines how human paternal behavior compares with that of other species and how it varies across human societies.

Armin A. Brott's "The New Father: A Dad's Guide to the First Year" offers practical advice and explores the emotional, financial, and physical changes a new father might experience.

"The Role of the Father in Child Development," edited by Michael E. Lamb, is a seminal work that compiles research on the father's role across various developmental stages of a child's life. It offers insights into how fathers contribute to their children's emotional, social, and cognitive development.

"Do Fathers Matter? What Science Is Telling Us About the Parent We've Overlooked" by Paul Raeburn - Raeburn synthesizes a wide range of scientific research to argue for fathers' significant impact on their children, from conception through adulthood.

Gillian Ranson's "Fathering: Masculinity and the Embodiment of Care" explores how men negotiate their identities as fathers and caregivers within the context of societal expectations about masculinity and fatherhood.

Jeremy A. Smith's "The Daddy Shift: How Stay-at-Home Dads, Breadwinning Moms, and Shared Parenting Are Transforming the American Family" discusses the changing dynamics of American families. It focuses on the rise of stay-at-home dads and how these shifts challenge traditional notions of fatherhood and masculinity.

Academic Papers

"The Effects of Father Involvement: An Updated Research Summary of the Evidence" by Sarah Allen and Kerry Daly - This paper summarizes recent research findings on the impact of father involvement on children and families, highlighting the positive benefits of active fathering.

"Involved Fatherhood and Men's Adult Development: Provisional Balances" by Michael E. Lamb examines the impact of fatherhood on men's development, arguing that active involvement in parenting leads to positive outcomes for fathers.

"Masculinities and Fatherhood: The Case of Fair and Equal Parenting" by Andrea Doucet - Doucet explores how fathers who engage in "fair and equal parenting" navigate and negotiate their masculinities within the context of their family lives.

"Paternal Participation in Child Care and Its Effects on Children's Self-Esteem and Attitudes toward Gendered Roles" by Elizabeth Thomson, Sara McLanahan, and Robert L. Hanson - This study investigates how fathers' involvement in child care influences children's self-esteem and their perceptions of gender roles.

"Gender and Parenthood: Biological and Social Scientific Perspectives" edited by W. Bradford Wilcox and Kathleen Kovner Kline - This collection of essays examines how biology and social science intersect to shape parenting practices and gender roles within families.

Journal of Family Psychology: Offers research on family dynamics and roles.

Fathering: A Journal of Theory, Research, and Practice about Men as Fathers: This journal focuses explicitly on fatherhood and can provide insights into how the role of fathers is viewed and studied academically.

These works contribute to a deeper understanding of fatherhood and parenting's multifaceted nature within various societal and cultural contexts. They offer valuable insights for scholars, students, and anyone interested in the dynamics of family life and gender roles. They combine scholarly research, practical advice, personal experiences, and theoretical exploration to comprehensively view the factors influencing fathers' roles in different contexts.

ACKNOWLEDGEMENTS

As this book comes to fruition, we sincerely appreciate and respect the contributions of several key organizations and individuals whose work and dedication have inspired and shaped this narrative's essence.

Firstly, we extend our heartfelt gratitude to the **Phoenix Local Organizing Committee (PHXLOC)**, whose relentless commitment to community empowerment and social justice in Phoenix has been a beacon of hope and invaluable insights for this work. Your efforts to uplift the community set a profound example of collective action and solidarity.

The **Our Black Fathers Community (OBFC)** deserves special mention for its pivotal role in reshaping the narrative around Black fatherhood. Your dedication to celebrating and supporting Black fathers has highlighted the joys, challenges, and resilience inherent in Black paternity. Your efforts, constant engagement, support, and experiences and our brotherhood fellowship have immeasurably enriched this book.

To **Mark Perlman, MA**, the creator of the **Nurturing Fathers Program**, your visionary work in fatherhood education and support has opened new pathways for understanding and embracing fathers' transformative role. Your program's principles and outcomes have been a guiding light, underscoring the importance of nurturing care in father-child relationships.

The **M.A.N. C.A.V.E.** and its creator, **Marion Hill**, as a mentor and guide, your wisdom, encouragement, and unwavering support have been invaluable. Your dedication to fostering positive change in individuals and communities has inspired this work and left an indelible mark on our personal and professional journeys. The **M.A.N. C.A.V.E.** initiative deserves recognition for its innovative approach to creating safe spaces for men to discuss, reflect, and grow. The commitment to mental health and emotional well-being among men has been a vital resource, reminding us of the strength found in vulnerability and community.

Additionally, we thank the **City of Phoenix Head Start Birth to Five program**, the **Greater Phoenix Urban League**, and **My Brother's Keeper**. Each organization has played a significant role in supporting families and youth, contributing to the broader context in which this book was conceived. Your collective missions and achievements have provided critical perspectives on our communities' challenges and opportunities today.

This book is a testament to the above-mentioned people's collective wisdom, resilience, and dedication. We hope it honors your contributions and furthers our mission of uplifting and empowering fathers and families across communities.

AUTHOR THURSTON M. SMITH

Thurston M. Smith, the world's number one Alpha Gentleman Lifestyle Development educator, is a multifaceted individual whose diverse roles and accomplishments paint the picture of a leader deeply committed to fostering growth, understanding, and unity. As the Economic Empowerment chair of the Greater Phoenix Urban League Youth Professionals in Phoenix, AZ., Thurston has demonstrated exceptional acumen in managing financial strategies to support community programs and initiatives. However, his true passion, his driving force, lies in empowering fathers. Thurston is a facilitator and educator in behavioral health who is determined to make a difference, ignite a spark of change in fathers and help them become the best versions of themselves. His mission is to empower fathers to break the cycle of outdated parenting practices, foster healthier relationships, enhance their communication skills, and cultivate greater emotional intelligence. Thurston conducts thought-provoking workshops, impactful seminars, and personalized consultations to achieve this, inspiring fathers to take the first step toward a better future for their families.

Thurston's entrepreneurial prowess and knack for fostering relationships are best exemplified in his role as the president and co-founder of Smoke & Sip International. With his business partner and close friend, Jaimel D. Hill, Thurston has crafted a unique platform for cigar aficionados and enthusiasts worldwide. This venture is not just a business but a testament to Thurston's distinct approach to entrepreneurship, which values meaningful connections and shared experiences above all.

Thurston's unwavering commitment to his family is the bedrock of his life. As a loving father and devoted husband, he actively engages in youth sports coaching, imparting the values of teamwork, respect, and perseverance. His passion for community building and outreach is palpable in his hands-on approach to supporting and uplifting those around him.

As an accomplished Leadership Coach, Speaker, Author, and Consultant, Thurston translates complex concepts into accessible, actionable insights. His journey in the speaking industry began with a notable accolade at the Maricopa Big Speak Out, where he received his first award for an informative speech. This recognition fueled his passion for Leadership Development and Effective Communication, leading him to a career where he empowers men to embrace their roles with clarity, pride, and refined principles.

Thurston's contributions have earned him significant recognition. Toastmasters International honored him for his transformative influence on how men perceive and fulfill their roles within the family and the broader community. His work is characterized by a genuine commitment to catalyzing positive change, fueled by his deep pride in his Belize heritage, which shapes and enriches his perspective and approach to leadership and community engagement.

In essence, Thurston M. Smith is a dynamic force for positive change and a beacon of leadership. His life and work embody the principles of leadership, community service, and family values. His ongoing journey is a beacon of inspiration, underscoring the power of dedicated, principled action in shaping a better world for future generations. His leadership is not just about guiding others but about leading by example, inspiring others to follow in his footsteps and make a difference in their spheres of influence.

AUTHOR JAIMEL D. HILL

Jaimel D. Hill, a US Army veteran from Pittsburg, California, is multitalented. He is a dedicated father, loving husband, and dynamic serial entrepreneur with a portfolio of successful businesses and partnerships. With over two decades of experience, Mr. Hill has made significant strides in strength and conditioning, serving as a performance trainer and multi-sport coach at the youth, high school, and college levels.

His journey took a transformative turn in 2016 when he expanded his expertise into life coaching and established the brand #DBWT—Don't Be Wasted Talent. This brand embodies his commitment to preventing wasted potential and fostering purpose-driven lives. Under his guidance, numerous mentees have reached prestigious heights in various fields, including the NFL, NBA, military, and other notable professions like coaching, law enforcement, fire & rescue, and teaching.

Mr. Hill's influence extends beyond individual mentorship; he actively contributes to community development by participating in nonprofit boards and founding his 501(c)3 organization, Youth Dreams To Reality, which empowers young individuals to achieve their aspirations.

In his affiliations, Mr. Hill is an integral part of Catch The Vision Ministry, M.A.N C.A.V.E and Our Black Fathers Committee (OBFC). As a mentee of Alpha Gentleman Lifestyle Development under Thurston M. Smith's mentorship and as a certified facilitator of the Nurturing Fathers Program by Mark Perlman, MA, he imparts essential parenting and nurturing skills to men, reinforcing his commitment to positive community impact.

In the business realm, Mr. Hill is the Vice President of Smoke & Sip International, a business networking organization that caters to cigar enthusiasts and entrepreneurs. His role is pivotal in driving operations, spearheading content creation for social media monetization and growth, organizing events, and contributing to the development of S&S LLC as a distinguished boutique cigar brand.

Mr. Hill's accolades and contributions to his community and beyond illustrate a legacy of leadership, mentorship, and entrepreneurial success. His life's work is a testament to his unwavering dedication to fostering talent and nurturing the next generation of leaders and innovators. He continues to inspire and lead with a clear vision and purpose, shaping a brighter future for individuals and communities.

APPENDICES A-K

HERITAGE UNVEILED: SCHOLARLY INTROSPECTIONS ON THE RAMIFICATIONS OF FATHERHOOD

This appendix presents a curated collection of book reports that delve deeply into the themes of fatherhood, raising children, and navigating the societal challenges Black fathers face in America. Each book, authored by influential Black American writers, offers rich experiences, insights, and guidance on the role of fatherhood within the Black community. From personal narratives and survival workbooks to academic research and cultural analyses, these works illuminate Black fathers' joys, struggles, and resilience as they endeavor to guide their children through a society rife with racial and social complexities.

The selection aims to provide readers with a deeper, comprehensive understanding of the dynamics at play in the lives of Black fathers and their families. It highlights the importance of fatherly love, the impact of societal perceptions, and the strategies for fostering strong, empowered children capable of overcoming the barriers they may face. Through this collection, we hope to challenge stereotypes, celebrate the profound contributions of Black fathers to their families and communities, and offer valuable resources for anyone interested in the crucial subject of fatherhood in the context of Black American experiences.

As you explore these book reports, we invite you to reflect on the diverse perspectives and lessons contained within each work. Whether you are a father, a mother, an educator, or simply someone interested in the broader societal implications of parenting in the Black community, this collection promises to enlighten, inspire, and provoke thoughtful discussion on the essence and evolution of Black fatherhood in America.

APPENDIX A

DR. NA'IM AKBAR

"VISIONS FOR BLACK MEN"

Introduction:

"Visions for Black Men" by Dr. Na'im Akbar is a profound exploration of African American men's psychological, historical, and cultural journey through the ages. Dr. Akbar, a renowned psychologist with deep insights into the African American experience, crafts a narrative that is both enlightening and empowering, aiming to redefine Black men's identity in a historically marginalized society. This book not only confronts the challenges faced by Black men but also celebrates their resilience, strength, and the pivotal role they play in the fabric of their communities and beyond.

Summary:

Dr. Akbar's work is divided into sections that tackle various aspects of the Black male experience, starting with a historical overview that traces the roots of African civilizations and the disintegration of Black male identity through the horrors of slavery and systemic racism. He discusses the psychological impact of these historical traumas and the ongoing struggle against the stereotypes and constraints imposed by a predominantly white society.

The concept of self-discovery is central to the book. Dr. Akbar encourages Black men to embark on a journey of self-exploration, urging them to shed the negative images and roles prescribed by an oppressive system. He emphasizes the importance of understanding their rich cultural heritage and the legacies of strength, wisdom, and leadership inherent in their ancestry.

"Visions for Black Men" also delves into Black men's roles in their families and communities. Dr. Akbar highlights the significance of positive male role models and the critical impact of fatherhood, brotherhood, and mentorship in nurturing the next generation. He calls for a collective effort to rebuild and reinforce the bonds within the Black community, advocating for unity, mutual support, and reclaiming their rightful place in society.

Analysis:

Dr. Akbar's insightful analysis is backed by his extensive knowledge of psychology and deep understanding of African American culture. His writing is both accessible and academically rigorous, offering readers a comprehensive view of the issues. One of the book's strengths is its ability to blend historical context with practical advice, making it a valuable resource for those seeking to understand the complexities of Black masculinity and for Black men aspiring to realize their full potential.

However, while Visions for Black Men is focused on the African American male experience, the themes of resilience, self-discovery, and community responsibility resonate universally. The book challenges readers to reflect on the societal structures that shape racial identities and how we can all contribute to a more just and equitable world.

"Visions for Black Men" by Dr. Na'im Akbar offers a wealth of insights and guidance for understanding and improving the lives of Black men within the context of their unique historical, cultural, and societal position. Here are some of the key highlights and important takeaways from the book:

- *Embracing African Heritage:* **Rediscovery of Roots:** Akbar emphasizes the importance of Black men reconnecting with their African heritage and understanding the rich history and civilizations from which they originate. This connection fosters a sense of pride, identity, and strength.

- *Overcoming Psychological Barriers:* **Shedding Negative Stereotypes:** The book challenges Black men to reject the negative stereotypes and limitations imposed by systemic racism and societal expectations. Akbar encourages cultivating a positive self-image based on the resilience, wisdom, and leadership inherent in African American history.

- *The Power of Education and Self-Development:* **Lifelong Learning:** Education is presented as a key tool for empowerment. Akbar stresses the importance of formal education and self-directed learning in achieving personal growth, community development, and socio-economic advancement.

· *The Role in Family and Community:* **Leadership and Responsibility** Akbar delineates the critical role of Black men as leaders in their families and communities. He advocates for active participation in fatherhood, mentorship, and community service as pathways to rebuild and strengthen communal bonds.

· *Unity and Collective Work:* **Community Solidarity:** One of the book's central themes is the power of unity and collaboration. Akbar calls for Black men to work to-gether to address social issues, support one another's growth, and collectively uplift the African American community.

· *Mental Health and Emotional Well-being:* **Healing from Trauma:** Akbar acknowledges the historical and on-going traumas faced by Black men and discusses the importance of mental health and emotional well-being. He encourages seeking healing through therapy, spiri-tual practices, and community support.

· *Constructing Positive Male Identity:* **Redefining Mascu-linity:** The book invites Black men to redefine what masculinity means to them beyond the constraints of traditional gender roles and societal expectations. It promotes a masculinity that is nurturing, vulnerable, and responsible.

· *Social Activism and Advocacy:* **Fighting for Justice:** Akbar underscores the importance of social activism and the fight against racial injustice. He inspires Black men to advocate for change, not only for their rights but also for the betterment of society.

· *Spiritual Growth:* **Spiritual Connection:** The book also touches on the significance of spiritual growth and connection as foundations for personal development and community leadership.

Conclusion:

"Visions for Black Men" is more than just a book; it is a call to action and a source of inspiration. Dr. Na'im Akbar provides a roadmap for healing and growth for Black men and the entire African American community. His vision is empowerment, unity, and the reclamation of greatness obscured by centuries of oppression. This work is a testament to Black men's enduring spirit and indomitable strength, offering hope and direction for future generations. It is a must-read for anyone committed to understanding and supporting the journey toward racial equality and personal transformation.

APPENDIX B

TA-NEHISI COATES

"BETWEEN THE WORLD AND ME"

"Between the World and Me," penned by Ta-Nehisi Coates, is a powerful letter to his teenage son, Samori. It unfolds as a deeply personal narrative, yet encapsulating the collective experience of being Black in America. Coates weaves history, personal revelation, and a poignant exploration of the American dream through a father's concern for his son in a society where Black bodies are vulnerable.

Summary:

Structured as a letter, Coates's book is a candid, reflective dialogue that spans America's racial divide's personal and historical landscapes. It navigates through Coates's experiences, from the streets of Baltimore to the historical significance of Howard University, which he refers to as "The Mecca." Through his journey, Coates confronts the realities of systemic racism, the false promise of the American dream to Black Americans, and the perpetual fear for his son's safety in a country marked by racial injustice.

Themes of Fatherhood:

At its heart, the book is a father's attempt to articulate the complexities of his identity and heritage to his son. Coates's narrative is imbued with a sense of duty to prepare Samori for navigating a world that is often hostile to Black bodies. The themes of fatherhood are interlaced with a stark realism about the dangers his son faces, coupled with an unwavering love and hope for his future. This duality captures the essence of African American fatherhood—the constant balance between imparting harsh truths and nurturing hope.

Societal Reflections:

"Between the World and Me" mirrors the deeply ingrained racial prejudices and systemic injustices of American society. Coates challenges the reader to confront these realities, not through abstract theories but through a Black father's tangible fears and hopes for his child. His narrative underscores the importance of understanding and acknowledging America's racial history to pave the way for a more equitable future.

Connection to "To Be One He Has To See One":

Integrating Coates's exploration of fatherhood into "To Be One He Has To See One" enriches the dialogue on the transformative power of fatherhood. Coates's candid portrayal of his fears and hopes and the lessons he wishes to impart to his son resonates with the broader themes of guiding a boy to manhood amidst societal challenges. His work exemplifies the role of a father as both a protector and educator, navigating the complexities of identity and race, making it a crucial addition to the conversation on righteous manhood.

Conclusion:

"Between the World and Me" by Ta-Nehisi Coates is not just an exploration of the Black experience in America; it is a profound discourse on the realities of fatherhood within that context. Coates offers insights into African American fathers' fears, hopes, and responsibilities through his heartfelt letter to his son. His narrative is a crucial voice in the ongoing dialogue about race, identity, and fatherhood in America, making it an essential read for anyone seeking to understand the depth and nuance of these interconnected experiences.

ETAN THOMAS & NICK CHILES

"FATHERHOOD: RISING TO THE ULTIMATE CHALLENGE"

Introduction:

"Fatherhood: Rising to the Ultimate Challenge" by Etan Thomas with Nick Chiles is not merely a book; it is an urgent call to reexamine the narrative surrounding Black fatherhood in America. Through personal anecdotes, interviews, and reflections, Thomas and Chiles navigate the reader through the experiences of being a Black father today. This book serves as both a mirror and a beacon, reflecting the diverse realities of Black fathers and illuminating the path toward a more inclusive and accurate understanding of their role.

Summary:

At its core, the book dismantles the monolithic stereotype of the absent Black father, presenting a wide range of experiences that celebrate involvement, love, and the challenges Black men face in their quest to be good fathers. Thomas, drawing from his journey and the insights of others—including prominent figures such as Kareem Abdul-Jabbar, Tony Dungy, and Talib Kweli—offers a deeply personal and universally resonant narrative. The stories shared within these pages span the spectrum of fatherhood, from the trials of co-parenting and dealing with the legal system to the joys of mentoring and shaping their children's futures.

Impactful Themes:

One of the book's most compelling themes is the challenge of navigating societal expectations and systemic barriers that uniquely impact Black fathers. Thomas and Chiles delve into how economic disparities, racial discrimination, and cultural stereotypes complicate the fatherhood journey. However, amidst these challenges, the book spotlights the resilience and creativity with which these fathers build meaningful relationships with their children.

Another critical theme is the evolution of Black masculinity and the embrace of vulnerability as strength. The authors argue that true strength in fatherhood lies in emotional presence, open communication, and the courage to be vulnerable. This redefinition of masculinity challenges traditional norms and offers a more holistic model of what it means to be a strong Black man and father.

Connection to Broader Conversations:

"Fatherhood: Rising to the Ultimate Challenge" contributes significantly to the broader conversation about fathers' societal roles. By highlighting the specific experiences of Black fathers, Thomas and Chiles provide valuable insights into the broader dynamics of family, community, and societal growth. Their narrative reinforces the idea that fatherhood is a critical factor in societal health and that supporting fathers in their roles is essential for the well-being of future generations.

Conclusion:

Etan Thomas and Nick Chiles's "Fatherhood: Rising to the Ultimate Challenge" is a powerful testament to Black fatherhood's complexity, joy, and significance. It challenges stereotypes, offers hope, and calls for a deeper understanding and support of Black fathers. The book is essential for anyone interested in family dynamics, parenting challenges in the face of systemic barriers, and the beauty of fatherly love and guidance. As it weaves together the personal and the universal, it invites readers to reflect on their perceptions of fatherhood and appreciate the diverse ways fathers rise to the ultimate challenge.

APPENDIX D

HILL HARPER

"THE CONVERSATION: HOW BLACK MEN AND WOMEN CAN BUILD LOVING, TRUSTING RELATIONSHIPS"

Introduction:

In the compelling work "The Conversation," Hill Harper embarks on a mission to explore and mend the complex dynamics between Black men and women in America. Through candid narratives, statistical insights, and personal reflections, Harper dissects the layers of relationship challenges within the Black community and provides a roadmap toward understanding, healing, and growth. This book is a critical call to action, urging Black men and women to engage in open, honest dialogues to build stronger, more resilient relationships.

Impact and Influence

"The Conversation" illuminates the often-unspoken realities that influence Black relationships. Harper addresses issues ranging from economic pressures and societal expectations to the impact of historical trauma, creating a comprehensive picture of Black couples' challenges. However, this book is set apart by Harper's unyielding optimism and actionable advice.

Harper champions a proactive approach to overcoming obstacles and fostering love and trust by encouraging personal accountability, empathy, and mutual respect.

Call to Action

This book is not just a passive observation of the state of Black relationships in America; it is a vibrant call to action. Harper implores readers to break the cycle of silence and misunderstanding that too often leads to hurt and division. He advocates for a new "The Conversation" era – a sustained, open dialogue prioritizing understanding and compassion over conflict and detachment. Harper's message is clear: building loving, trusting relationships is not only possible but essential for the well-being of the Black community.

Why This Matters

In a society where Black relationships are often depicted through a lens of stereotype and struggle, "The Conversation" offers a much-needed counter-narrative. Harper's focus on communication and understanding highlights the power of vulnerability and the importance of seeing beyond societal constructs to the heart of individual experience. This book is essential for anyone who fosters healthier relationships and a stronger community.

Your Role in "The Conversation"

As readers, our role extends beyond the pages of this book. We are invited to participate actively in "The Conversation," applying Harper's insights to our lives and communities. This means engaging in honest dialogues with partners, friends, and family members and working collectively to address the challenges that Harper outlines. It is about taking personal responsibility for the health of our relationships and, by extension, the strength of our community.

Conclusion

"The Conversation: How Black Men and Women Can Build Loving, Trusting Relationships" is more than a book; it is a movement toward healing and unity within the Black community. Hill Harper offers not just a critique but a solution, a way forward that requires courage, honesty, and a commitment to change. Let this book catalyze your conversations, a starting point for building the loving, trusting relationships that Harper envisions. The journey begins with us, one conversation at a time.

PATRICIA JOSEPH

"RAISING BLACK BOYS TO MEN: A MOTHER'S GUIDE TO RAISING THUGLESS SONS"

Introduction

In the thought-provoking and deeply insightful book, "Raising Black Boys to Men: A Mother's Guide to Raising Thugless Sons," Patricia Joseph offers a compelling exploration into the challenges and triumphs of rearing African American males in a society that often harbors preconceived notions and systemic barriers against them. Grounded in psychological research and infused with the author's personal experiences, Joseph's work serves as both a guide and a clarion call to parents and guardians dedicated to nurturing young Black boys into successful, resilient men.

Summary of Key Points

Joseph's narrative is structured around the central themes of identity, societal expectations, and the unique challenges Black boys face from childhood through adolescence. She delves into the psychological impact of racial stereotyping and systemic discrimination, detailing how these forces can shape a young boy's self-perception and worldview.

One of the book's strengths is its evidence-based approach to discussing the developmental needs of Black boys. Joseph references many studies highlighting the importance of positive male role models, educational disparities' impact, and societal labeling's effects on psychological development. She advocates for a nurturing and assertive parenting style, emphasizing the need for open communication, emotional support, and setting high expectations to counteract negative societal messages.

Joseph also addresses the critical role of the community in raising children, underscoring the African proverb, "It takes a village to raise a child." She emphasizes the importance of community support systems, mentorship programs, and educational resources in providing Black boys with a broader network of positive influences and opportunities.

Analysis and Reflection

"Raising Black Boys to Men" stands out for its candid and heartening message, bolstered by scientific research and psychological insights. Joseph masterfully bridges the gap between personal anecdotes and academic data, making a compelling case for a proactive and love-centered approach to parenting. The book challenges readers to look beyond societal stereotypes and cultivate environments that promote growth, learning, and resilience.

However, while the book is a powerful resource for parents of Black boys, its title and focus might unintentionally alienate potential readers who could benefit from its messages, such as educators, mentors, and even parents of children of other races. Expanding the audience could foster broader societal change in perceptions and interactions with Black males.

Societal Implications

Joseph's work is a timely contribution to the ongoing race, parenting, and societal change discourse. By providing a science-based, psychological framework for understanding the unique challenges of raising Black boys, the book empowers parents and invites society to reevaluate its role in supporting or hindering the development of its young members. The book implicitly argues for systemic reforms in education, criminal justice, and social services to create a more equitable society for Black boys to grow into men.

Conclusion

"Raising Black Boys to Men: A Mother's Guide to Raising Thugless Sons" is a seminal work that combines rigorous research with a passionate plea for understanding and action. Patricia Joseph illuminates the path for parents navigating the complexities of raising Black boys in America and offers valuable insights into the societal changes necessary to ensure these boys can grow into confident, booming, and respected men. This book is essential for anyone invested in the future of Black boys and the society that molds them.

APPENDIX F

JORDAN THIERRY

"THE BLACK FATHERHOOD PROJECT:

LEGACY AND LOVE"

Introduction:

In "The Black Fatherhood Project: Legacy and Love," Jordan Thierry embarks on a groundbreaking exploration of the multifaceted experience of Black fatherhood in America. This compelling book, an extension of the documentary that shares its name, delves deep into the historical, social, and emotional landscapes that Black fathers navigate. Thierry's work is not just a book but a powerful testament to Black fathers' resilience, love, and legacy amidst a society riddled with stereotypes and systemic challenges.

Summary:

At its core, "The Black Fatherhood Project" is a narrative of triumph and tenderness. Thierry meticulously unravels the threads of history, culture, and personal experience to paint a rich portrait of Black fatherhood. Through interviews, research, and personal reflections, he sheds light on the joys and struggles of Black fathers, from the dehumanizing narratives spun during the era of slavery to the persistent stereotypes in contemporary media.

The book is structured around legacy—how past generations of Black men have navigated fatherhood and how these legacies inform and inspire today's fathers. Thierry weaves together stories of love that defy the odds, offering readers a glimpse into the intimate moments that define father-child relationships. These stories serve as a counter-narrative to the prevailing myths of absentee Black fathers, highlighting instead their profound commitment to nurturing and guiding their children.

Impactful Themes:

One of the most striking themes in Thierry's work is the transformative power of love. Despite facing societal barriers and enduring personal sacrifices, the fathers featured in this book demonstrate unwavering passion and dedication to their families. Their stories illuminate the complex interplay between vulnerability and strength, showing that at the heart of Black fatherhood is an unrelenting love that fuels resilience and hope.

Thierry also tackles the issue of systemic challenges head-on, from the economic disparities that disproportionately affect Black families to the criminal justice system that has torn countless fathers from their homes. However, even within these discussions, the focus remains on the agency and creativity of Black fathers in overcoming these obstacles to be present and engaged in their children's lives.

Jaw-Dropping Insights:

Perhaps the most jaw-dropping aspect of Thierry's work is the revelation of the sheer diversity within Black fatherhood. The book dismantles monolithic stereotypes by showcasing the wide variety of ways Black men embody fatherhood—whether they are single fathers, co-parenting, adoptive fathers, or father figures within their communities. Each narrative brings a unique perspective, collectively painting a vibrant mosaic of what it means to be a Black father in America.

Conclusion:

"The Black Fatherhood Project: Legacy and Love" is a seminal work that challenges, educates, and inspires. Jordan Thierry has crafted a book and created a movement that celebrates Black fathers' strength, love, and resilience. This book is a clarion call to recognize and honor their vital role in shaping the next generation. It leaves readers with a renewed understanding of the complexities of Black fatherhood and a profound appreciation for the men who rise every day to the call of fatherhood, armed with love and legacy. In the end, Thierry's book is more than just a read; it is an experience that changes the way we see the world, compelling us to look beyond stereotypes and appreciate the depth and diversity of the Black fatherhood experience.

APPENDIX G

JEFF HOBBS

"VISIBLE MAN: A STORY OF POST-RACIST AMERICA"

Overview

"Visible Man: A True Story of Post-Racist America" by Jeff Hobbs is a compelling exploration of race, identity, and fatherhood in what the author terms "post-racist" America. Through the life story of Rodney King, not the victim of the infamous police beating but a man sharing the same name, Hobbs crafts a narrative that delves deep into the complexities and challenges that Black men and fathers face in contemporary society. The book is a personal account and a broader societal study, offering insights into how race continues to shape experiences, opportunities, and perceptions in the United States.

Analysis

Hobbs uses the story of Rodney King as a lens to examine the nuanced realities of living as a Black man in America today. King's journey, marked by personal triumphs and setbacks, becomes a powerful illustration of the broader struggles and resilience of Black fathers striving to provide for and protect their families in a world that often seems stacked against them.

Hobbs meticulously documents King's efforts to navigate societal expectations, economic challenges, and the ever-present undercurrents of racial prejudice, offering readers a raw and unfiltered glimpse into his life.

The notion of a "post-racist" America is critically examined through King's experiences. Hobbs challenges the optimistic narrative of racial progress, highlighting the persistent disparities and systemic obstacles that Black individuals and families continue to encounter. The book's title, "Visible Man," is a play on Ralph Ellison's "Invisible Man," suggesting a shift from the invisibility of Black Americans to a state where their struggles are acknowledged but not necessarily facilitated by society.

Themes

One of the book's central themes is the enduring power of fatherhood. Hobbs portrayed King's role as a father, his aspirations for his children, and his determination to break the cycle of disenfranchisement that has historically plagued Black families in America with depth and empathy. Hobbs illuminated the significance of fatherhood as a source of hope, strength, and legacy in the Black community while acknowledging the immense pressures that come with it.

Another prominent theme is visibility and its double-edged nature. For King and many Black fathers, visibility means recognizing their humanity and challenges, yet it also subjects them to scrutiny, judgment, and vulnerability. Hobbs skillfully navigates this paradox, presenting visibility as a physical state and a complex social and psychological phenomenon.

Impact and Relevance

"Visible Man" is a profoundly influential work that sheds light on the realities of race and fatherhood in modern America. Jeff Hobbs has created a narrative that is a personal story and a social commentary, resonating with readers across diverse backgrounds. By focusing on the life of Rodney King, Hobbs offers a nuanced perspective on the challenges and triumphs of Black fatherhood, contributing to the ongoing dialogue about race, equality, and justice in the United States.

The book's exploration of the themes of visibility, identity, and the enduring significance of fatherhood makes it an essential read for anyone seeking to understand the complexities of navigating race and parenting in today's society. "Visible Man: A True Story of Post-Racist America" is not just a reflection on the state of race relations but a call to acknowledge, engage with, and address the deep-seated issues that continue to affect Black Americans.

Conclusion

In "Visible Man," Jeff Hobbs has crafted a powerful and poignant exploration of the lives of Black fathers in America, challenging readers to confront the realities of a society far from post-racial. Through the story of Rodney King, the book offers a unique insight into the struggles and resilience of Black men striving to fulfill their roles as fathers amid systemic challenges. This work contributes significantly to the conversation about race, identity, and fatherhood, offering hope and highlighting the importance of visibility, understanding, and change.

DAVID MILLER

"DARE TO BE KING: WHAT IF THE PRINCE LIVES? A SURVIVAL WORKBOOK FOR AFRICAN AMERICAN MALES"

Introduction

In the pivotal work "Dare to Be King: What If the Prince Lives? A Survival Workbook for African American Males," David Miller embarks on a profound journey to address the urgent challenges faced by African American boys and young men. This workbook is not merely a guide but a beacon of hope, strategy, and empowerment aimed at one of the most vulnerable demographics in American society. Through personal insights, practical exercises, and compelling narratives, Miller constructs a manual designed to equip young Black males with the tools necessary for survival, success, and self-realization in a society that often sets them up for failure.

Summary

At its core, "Dare to Be King" challenges and inspires its readers to envision a world where young Black males survive and thrive amidst adversities. Miller meticulously outlines a 52-week program, each focusing on a different theme or challenge, ranging from emotional intelligence and conflict resolution to financial literacy and academic achievement. The workbook format encourages active engagement, making the reader a participant in their journey of self-discovery and empowerment.

Impactful Themes

One of the book's most influential themes is the concept of "survival." However, Miller expands this notion beyond physical survival, delving into psychological, emotional, and spiritual survival. He addresses the systemic obstacles African American males face, including racial profiling, educational disparities, and economic exclusion, and offers tangible strategies to navigate and overcome these barriers.

Another pivotal theme is "identity." Miller prompts readers to explore and affirm their identity beyond societal stereotypes and expectations. "Dare to Be King" empowers young men to define themselves on their terms through exercises designed to foster a positive self-image and a strong sense of self-worth.

Societal Implications

Miller's workbook directly confronts the societal structures that contribute to the marginalization of African American males. By providing a roadmap for personal growth and resilience, "Dare to Be King" implicitly calls for a reevaluation of these structures. The book serves as a critical resource for educators, mentors, and community leaders, offering a framework to support the holistic development of young Black men.

Personal Reflections

"Dare to Be King" is more than an educational tool; it is a transformative experience. The workbook's practical exercises, coupled with Miller's compassionate and insightful guidance, challenge readers to confront their fears, acknowledge their potential, and embark on self-improvement and community leadership.

Conclusion

David Miller's "Dare to Be King: What If the Prince Lives? A Survival Workbook for African American Males" is a monumental contribution to the race, masculinity, and youth empowerment discourse. It is a call to action, a source of inspiration, and a manual for change. In addressing African American males' specific needs and challenges, Miller not only dares his readers to dream of a better future but also equips them with the skills to achieve it. This workbook transcends the personal, offering a blueprint for societal transformation—one young prince at a time.

APPENDIX I

JOE BREWSTER, MICHELE STEPHENSON, AND HILARY BEARD

"PROMISES KEPT: RAISING BLACK BOYS TO SUCCEED IN SCHOOL AND LIFE"

In a society where the narrative around Black masculinity often veers into stereotypes and misconceptions, "Promises Kept: Raising Black Boys to Succeed in School and Life" emerges as a beacon of hope, guidance, and actionable wisdom. Authored by Joe Brewster and Michele Stephenson, with Hilary Beard, this book extends the conversation initiated by their acclaimed documentary, "American Promise." It delves deep into the complexities, challenges, and joys of raising Black boys in America, offering personal insights, research-backed strategies, and practical advice for parents and communities alike.

Core Themes

At its heart, Promises Kept is about confronting and overcoming the systemic barriers that hinder Black boys' educational and personal development. The book is structured around the critical themes of identity, resilience, education, and parenting. Each section is meticulously designed to provide readers with a comprehensive understanding of Black boys' multifaceted challenges and the collective effort required to uplift them.

Insights and Strategies

One of the book's strengths lies in its honest portrayal of the author's experiences raising their son, Idris, alongside the stories of other families navigating similar paths. These narratives serve as powerful illustrations of the broader issues at play, from racial discrimination in educational systems to the psychological impacts of societal expectations on Black boys.

"Promises Kept" shines in its presentation of actionable strategies for empowering Black boys. It emphasizes the importance of creating supportive environments that affirm their identities, nurture their talents, and bolster their academic pursuits. The book advocates for active parental and community involvement and stresses the role of mentors, educators, and allies in fostering spaces where Black boys can thrive.

Community Engagement and Impact

"Promises Kept" is more than a book; it is a call to action for parents, educators, policymakers, and community members. The book challenges readers to engage in meaningful conversations about race, education, and parenting. Its comprehensive resource list, including organizations, books, and online platforms, encourages further exploration and involvement in initiatives supporting Black boys' success.

The book's impact extends beyond individual readers. It is a valuable resource for community groups, schools, and organizations dedicated to youth development. Hosting book clubs, workshops, and discussion forums centered around "Promises Kept" can stimulate dialogue, share best practices, and mobilize community efforts to support Black boys' growth and success.

Conclusion

"Promises Kept: Raising Black Boys to Succeed in School and Life" is an essential read for anyone invested in the well-being and future of Black boys. Through its compelling narratives, research-driven insights, and practical advice, the book offers a roadmap for nurturing resilient, educated, and empowered young men. In a world where the odds are often stacked against them, "Promises Kept" is a testament to Black boys' strength, potential, brilliance and the collective responsibility to uphold our promises to them.

Embracing the lessons of "Promises Kept," communities can create environments where Black boys survive and flourish. The journey toward equality and justice is long and fraught with challenges, but with commitment, understanding, and love, the promises made to Black boys can be kept, one child at a time.

This influential work does more than illuminate the barriers; it arms its readers with the knowledge and tools necessary to dismantle them. "Promises Kept" is not just a guide for raising Black boys; it is a transformative text that redefines the narrative around Black fatherhood, education, and community support. It stands as a pillar in the ongoing discourse on racial equality, pushing the envelope further by identifying problems and offering real, tangible solutions.

Expanding the Conversation

By engaging with "Promises Kept," communities are invited to expand the conversation on how societal structures —from schools to legal systems—impact the development of Black boys. The book lays bare the often unspoken realities these young men face, including racial profiling and unequal access to quality education, while also celebrating their resilience and achievements. It is a narrative that insists on hope and action in the same breath, urging communities to unite to ensure that Black boys have the same opportunities to succeed as their peers.

Building Networks of Support

"Promises Kept" highlights the critical role of support networks, emphasizing that the journey of raising Black boys to succeed is collective. It calls for creating supportive ecosystems that include parents, educators, mentors, and peers. These networks not only provide emotional and academic support but also act as buffers against the systemic inequalities that Black boys face. The book suggests practical ways communities can build these networks, from mentoring programs to parent-led initiatives that enhance educational opportunities.

Advocacy and Policy Change

Moreover, "Promises Kept" is a clarion call for advocacy and policy change. It challenges readers to work within their communities and engage in broader political and social action addressing racial inequality's root causes. The authors argue that real change for Black boys involves reforming the educational system, ensuring equitable access to resources, and dismantling the policies that perpetuate racial disparities. They provide a framework for advocacy, encouraging readers to become informed about the issues and to use their voices and votes to effect change.

Empowering Future Generations

Ultimately, "Promises Kept" is about empowerment—of Black boys, their families, and their communities. It envisions a world where Black boys are seen and valued for their potential, talents, and humanity. Through the collective efforts of all members of society, the book imagines a future where these boys can grow into men who are confident, educated, and empowered to achieve their dreams. It is a future where the societal promises of equality and justice are kept, and every Black boy can reach his fullest potential.

A Call to Read, Reflect, and Act

"Promises Kept: Raising Black Boys to Succeed in School and Life" is more than just essential reading; it is a resource that should be revisited and shared. As communities reflect on the insights and strategies outlined in the book, the call to action becomes clear: to act with intention and purpose to support Black boys in every aspect of their lives. By embracing the teachings of "Promises Kept," we can all contribute to a society that recognizes and actively champions Black boys' success and well-being.

APPENDIX J

FREEMAN A. HRABOWSKI, KENNETH I. MATON, AND GEOFFREY L. GREIF

"BEATING THE ODDS: RAISING ACADEMICALLY SUCCESSFUL AFRICAN AMERICAN MALES"

Introduction:

"Beating the Odds: Raising Academically Successful African American Males" by Freeman A. Hrabowski, Kenneth I. Maton, and Geoffrey L. Greif stands as a beacon of insight and guidance for anyone invested in the success and empowerment of young African American males. This seminal work delves into the complexities and challenges these young men face in their academic and personal lives and offers a roadmap for nurturing their potential against societal hurdles.

Summary:

At the heart of "Beating the Odds" is a compelling examination of the factors contributing to African American males' academic success. Drawing from extensive research and personal narratives, the authors highlight crucial elements such as family support, high expectations, racial identity, and the cultivation of resilience. The book is an academic treatise and a collection of stories of determination, guidance from mentors, and the transformative power of belief and support from family and community.

Correlation with "To Be One He Has To See One":

The themes and insights from "Beating the Odds" resonate deeply with those explored in "To Be One He Has To See One: The Only Way a Boy Becomes a Righteous Man." Both works underscore the critical role of fathers and father figures in shaping the lives of young men, particularly in the African American community. The premise that a boy must see a model of what he aspires to become aligns with the evidence and narratives presented by Hrabowski, Maton, and Greif, showcasing that visibility and representation are vital in nurturing the journey from boyhood to manhood.

Impactful Themes:

- Family and Community Support: "Beating the Odds" emphasizes the irreplaceable role of family, especially fathers, in setting high expectations and providing the emotional and psychological scaffolding for young men to thrive. This mirrors the principle in "To Be One He Has To See One" that the presence of a righteous man as a role model can profoundly influence a boy's path to becoming a similarly righteous adult.

- Resilience and Overcoming Adversity: Both books highlight the importance of resilience, a quality taught and caught from the example of fathers and male mentors. The stories of young men navigating through and overcoming societal and academic challenges in "Beating the Odds" serve as a testament to the strength and perseverance that can be cultivated within the supportive framework of fatherhood.

· The Power of Expectations: When communicated by fathers and mentors, the expectation of success motivates young men. "Beating the Odds" provides evidence that such expectations, alongside consistent support and guidance, can propel African American males toward academic and life success. This assertion echoes in "To Be One He Has To See One" that what fathers envision for their sons can shape their reality.

Relevance and Mind-Blowing Insight:

The relevance of "Beating the Odds" to the narrative of fatherhood and the molding of young men into righteous adults cannot be overstated. The book offers a mind-blowing insight into fathers and male figures' tangible impact on African American males' academic and overall life trajectories. It challenges readers to see beyond the statistics and recognize the individual potential within each young man. The correlation between this book and "To Be One He Has To See One" underscores a universal truth: the presence, involvement, and guidance of a father or a father figure are indispensable in helping a boy navigate the passage to manhood.

Conclusion:

"Beating the Odds: Raising Academically Successful African American Males" complements but deeply enriches the conversation initiated in "To Be One He Has To See One." Together, these works offer a compelling narrative on the transformative power of engaged fatherhood and the critical importance of male role models in the African American community. They serve as a call to action for all fathers, mentors, and communities to invest in young men's futures and guide them toward righteousness, resilience, and success.

APPENDIX K

CHARLES C. DANIELS JR.

& BERKELEY A. GORDON

"FATHERING WHILE BLACK: WISDOM, FEARS, HOPES, AND GUIDANCE FOR RAISING BLACK SONS IN AMERICA"

In the heart of a society that often seems to set them up for failure, Black fathers undertake a journey filled with immense love, deep fears, unyielding hope, and the profound desire to guide their sons through the complexities of life in America. "Fathering While Black" by Charles C. Daniels Jr. and Berkeley A. Gordon emerges not just as a book but as a beacon of strength, a source of wisdom, and a heartfelt call to arms for Black fathers everywhere. This powerful work dives into the heart of what it means to raise Black sons in a country where their skin color marks them from birth, enveloping readers in a narrative that is at once deeply personal and universally resonant.

Daniels and Gordon have crafted a masterful guide that transcends the traditional parenting book. Through a blend of personal anecdotes, psychological insights, and actionable advice, they lay bare the fears that haunt Black fathers—fears of violence, systemic injustice, and the myriad of obstacles their sons will face. Nevertheless, in the same breath, the authors illuminate the extraordinary hope that defines Black fatherhood: the hope for a brighter future, for doors opened wide, and for sons who rise above the constraints society attempts to place on them.

What sets "Fathering While Black" apart is its unflinching honesty. Daniels and Gordon do not shy away from the hard truths. They confront the stereotypes that shadow Black fathers—depictions of absenteeism and delinquency—and dismantle them with the reality of Black fathers' fierce commitment to their sons. The book is a testament to the countless Black fathers who pour their lives into nurturing, protecting, and teaching their sons, often against formidable odds.

Emotionally stirring and profoundly moving, "Fathering While Black" also offers a treasure trove of guidance. From navigating conversations about race to instilling resilience and pride in their heritage, Daniels and Gordon provide Black fathers with the tools they need to support their sons' growth into confident, conscious, and compassionate men. This guidance is grounded in recognizing Black fatherhood's unique beauty and strength and fathers' pivotal role in their sons' lives.

Perhaps the most soul-stirring aspect of the book is its celebration of the joys of Black fatherhood—the unbreakable bonds formed through shared laughter, lessons, and love. Daniels and Gordon invite readers into moments of tenderness and triumph that define the father-son relationship, showcasing fathers' profound impact on shaping their sons' identities and destinies.

In essence, "Fathering While Black" is more than a book; it is a journey through the heart of Black fatherhood. It speaks to the fears that whisper in the dead of night, the hopes that shine brightly even in the darkest times, and the unwavering love that binds fathers and sons. Daniels and Gordon have written a guide for Black fathers and penned a love letter to them, affirming their vital role in their sons' lives and the fabric of America.

For anyone seeking to understand the realities of Black fatherhood, to find solace in shared experiences, or to be inspired by the resilience and love that characterize it, "Fathering While Black" is an essential read. It is a book that stirs the soul, opens the heart, and reaffirms the power of fathers to shape the future, one son at a time.

BIBLIOGRAPHY

References:

1. Snyder, J. (2005). "Parenting Styles and Child Outcomes." *Journal of Family Psychology*, 19(2), 233-239. https://doi.org/10.1037/0893-3200.19.2.233. This article explores the correlation between different parenting styles and children's resulting behavioral and emotional outcomes, offering insights into effective parenting practices.

2. American Psychological Association (APA). (2012). "Developing Self-Regulation and Coping Skills." *American Psychological Association*. https://www.apa.org/research/action/childrens-coping-skills. This resource provides an overview of strategies and interventions to enhance self-regulation and coping mechanisms among children and adolescents.

3. NICHD Early Child Care Research Network. (2008). "Effects of Early Parenting on Children's Development." *National Institute of Child Health and Human Development*. https://www.nichd.nih.gov/research/supported/SECCYD. This comprehensive study examines the long-term impacts of early child care and parenting styles on children's development.

4. Pew Research Center. (2020). "Parenting in America Today." *Pew Research Center*. https://www.pewresearch.org/social-trends/2020/parenting-in-america-today/. This report presents findings from a national survey on the attitudes, concerns, and experiences of parents raising children in today's America, highlighting the challenges and rewards of parenting.

5. Thompson, M., & Kindlon, D. (2009). *Raising Cain: Protecting the Emotional Life of Boys*. Ballantine Books. ISBN 978-0345434852. This book discusses boys' emotional challenges and offers insights into fostering their emotional development, advocating for a more compassionate understanding of raising boys.

6. Lareau, A. (2011). *Unequal Childhoods: Class, Race, and Family Life*. University of California Press. ISBN 978-0520271425. Lareau's groundbreaking book offers an in-depth look at how socioeconomic status and race influence parenting styles and child development through detailed observations and analyses of American families.

7. Cabrera, N. J., Fitzgerald, H. E., Bradley, R. H., & Roggman, L. (2014). "The Ecology of Father-Child Relationships: An Expanded Model." *Journal of Family Theory & Review*, 6(4), 336-354. https://doi.org/10.1111/jftr.12054. This article proposes an expanded ecological model to understand father-child relationships, emphasizing the diverse contexts that shape these interactions and their effects on child development.

8. Bronfenbrenner, U., & Morris, P. A. (2006). "The Bioecological Model of Human Development." In W. Damon & R. M. Lerner (Eds.), *Handbook of Child Psychology* (6th ed., Vol. 1, pp. 793-828). Wiley. This foundational chapter outlines the bioecological model of human development, offering a comprehensive framework for understanding the complex interactions between individual, familial, and societal factors in child development.

9. Pruett, K. D. (2000). *Fatherneed: Why Father Care is as Essential as Mother Care for Your Child*. Broadway Books. ISBN 978-0767904843. Pruett's book delves into children's psychological and emotional needs for father involvement and outlines the critical roles fathers play in healthy child development.

10. Tamis-LeMonda, C. S., & Cabrera, N. (Eds.). (2002). *Handbook of Father Involvement: Multidisciplinary Perspectives*. Lawrence Erlbaum Associates. ISBN 978-0805837025. This comprehensive handbook combines research from various disciplines to explore

the multifaceted nature of father involvement and its impact on child development.

These references encompass books and peer-reviewed articles, providing a broader, multidisciplinary perspective on parenting, fatherhood, and child development. They are essential for anyone looking to understand the factors that influence the complex dynamics of family life and child upbringing.